A Doctor's Devotion

A Doctor's Devotion: A Passion for Serving
© 2012 Harry Holwerda
Published by Principia Media, LLC, Grand Rapids, MI
www.principiamedia.com

ISBN-13: 978-1-61485-311-4

Printed in the United States of America

18 17 16 15 14 13 12   7 6 5 4 3 2 1

Cover Design and Interior Layout: Frank Gutbrod

A Doctor's Devotion
A Passion for Serving

Dr. Harry Holwerda

PRINCIPIA
MEDIA

Introduction

Near the end of my medical school training in 1965, Joan and I had our first opportunity in medical missions. Three months before graduation I was able to serve an externship as a medical missionary in the jungles of South America. It was part of the medical work of the World Radio Missionary Fellowship in Ecuador. The work was among the Quechua and Jivaro Indians. The latter practiced the taking and shrinking the heads of their enemies. I also had incidental contact with the Auca Indians. Five missionaries had begun working with the Aucas nine years earlier. In a matter of weeks, they were killed by the Aucas in the jungle.

After graduation from the University of Michigan Medical School, I completed a rotating internship at Butterworth Hospital in Grand Rapids, Michigan. After finishing the internship, I volunteered for the United States Air Force. From 1966-1968 I completed two years of active duty during the Vietnam War. I was assigned to the flight surgeon's office at Andrews Air Force Base. There, I was granted presidential clearance and assigned flight duties as the president arrived and departed the base. In addition, I flew as the physician on longer flights for congressmen and the secretary of state.

Finishing my military service in June of 1968, my family and I left for Nigeria as representatives of Christian Reformed

World Missions. Civil war in Nigeria had begun the previous year. I was sent to a two hundred bed missionary hospital in southern Nigeria near the border of the French Cameroons. For the next two-and-a-half years, that would be our home.

In 1971, we returned to the United States. In July of that year, I began private practice with Dr. Roy Kingma, a college acquaintance, in DeMotte, Indiana. I practiced with him for fifteen years. In 1986, I returned to Grand Rapids, Michigan, and joined the larger private practice of Dr. John Maskill, Dr. Good, Dr. Barbara Wuerhman, and Dr. Newton. Dr. Taru Patel and Dr. Sal Dyke also joined us as others retired. I retired in 2005 after twenty years of medical practice with them.

After retirement, I began serving as a volunteer Medical Consultant with Christian Reformed World Missions. In 2008, I also served a year as the sole physician in a high security prison in my home state of Michigan. During the past twenty years my wife and I have continued to volunteer for several medical mission trips to Africa and Thailand.

> *"You know that those who are regarded as rulers of the Gentiles lord it over them, and their high officials exercise authority over them. Not so with you. Instead, whoever wants to become great among you must be your servant, and whoever wants to be first must be slave of all. For even the Son of Man did not come to be served, but to serve, and to give his life as a ransom for many."*
>
> MARK 10:42-45

Many in this world, perhaps most, wish to have a life with special privileges that include great wealth, power, influence, or authority. Many have difficulty in suppressing feelings of envy or even coveting the privileges of others. Many times we feel those privileges are undeserved, unearned, and obtained by being born with a "silver spoon" in their mouth. Why were we not so fortunate?

In the text from the Apostle Mark, Jesus completely altered what people should value in this world. He calls us instead to be the servants of others rather than having authority over them, to serve rather than to be served. The position He himself chose in His incarnation. For many, this call to service seems only a dreary call to a life of sacrifice.

Servants, after all, must be in total submission to their masters and available at all times to satisfy their wants and needs. Following Jesus' call to service may indeed require sacrifice. However, when we submit to Christ's call for service and we learn to value what He values, our lives are filled with unimaginable joys and blessings.

I have been a physician for most of my life. It is a vocation filled with opportunities for service. Physicians do not have to seek those in need. Those with physical, emotional, and spiritual needs will seek them. The past forty-five years practicing medicine have been a great privilege. Countless patients have invited me into their lives. They have come from every level of society and numerous cultural backgrounds. This medical journey has carried me to three continents and many countries. The majority of my patients have come from my own country. But I have been privileged to serve jungle Indians and headhunters, military personnel, those caught up among civil war in Africa, and those incarcerated in a high security prison. It has been an incredible medical journey. The devotions in this book, hopefully, will encourage and inspire you to live a life of service.

What do you most value in your life in this world? What best describes your view of life, to be served or to serve?

SEEING OPPORTUNITIES

"And pray in the spirit on all occasions with all kinds of prayers and requests."

EPHESIANS 6:18

In a busy medical practice, I often saw thirty or more patients a day. Time was precious. On the mission field, that number was even greater. How can a busy doctor effectively and kindly serve the physical and emotional needs of his patients, staff, family, and all the others he meets each day? How can he find time for the special individuals each day whose need for comfort, encouragement, or spiritual direction far exceed the needs of others?

As a Christian physician, I first tried to meet the physical and emotional needs of my patients. However, I also felt a deep concern for their spiritual welfare. I believe that sharing one's faith is best done by earning the right to do so. I did not "preach" to my patients or others. I did not speak to everyone. Rather as the Apostle Peter said, "...be prepared to give an answer to everyone who asks you to give the reason for the hope that you have. But do this with gentleness and respect." I Peter 3:15

How do you find opportunities where the sharing of faith becomes a natural part of the conversation and not something forced upon a captive or unwilling listener? My habit is to pray each night that God will place in my path one individual with a special need for comfort, encouragement, or the plan of salvation. Secondly, I pray that I would be sensitive to that need and prepared to meet it.

I call this efficient evangelism. I believe that God uses us. But first He uses the Holy Spirit to touch the heart of others so that they are able to hear the reason for the hope that is in us. It is efficient because it allows you to perform the work you have been called to do. You need not speak to everyone you see. It is effective, because you and God work together. It is necessary because II Corinthians 5:19-20 states, " that God was reconciling the world to himself in Christ, not counting people's sins against them. And that He has committed to us the message of reconciliation. We are therefore Christ's ambassadors..." Are you willing to be used by God? Pray for the opportunities, and be prepared to meet them daily. Many will be in unexpected situations and among those you would least expect to be interested.

A CALL TO MISSIONS

"In the same way, any of you who does not
give up everything, he cannot be my disciple..."

LUKE 14:33

I was nearing the end of four years of medical education at the University of Michigan. Before graduation I was scheduled for three months of elective activities. Eight months earlier, my wife Joan and I attended the Worldwide Medical Missionary Conference in Wheaton, Illinois. We had both thought deeply about medical mission work; she while completing a nursing degree and I in medical school.

Veteran missionary physicians from around the world attended the conference. We were excited and challenged as we listened to their experiences and heard of their sacrifices. Particularly touching was the account of the death of Dr. Paul Carlson in the Congo two months earlier. As rebels involved in the civil war approached his hospital, he refused to leave his patients. When they swept through the compound, he, along with many of his patients, was killed. The next day, those who came to rescue him found his camera lying next to his body. Pictures from the camera revealed the events leading up to his death. He was willing to give up everything, even his life, in his service to others.

At lunch that day we were invited to work for three months with Dr. Everett Fuller, a general surgeon, working in the rainforest of Ecuador. His mission employer, HCJB World Radio, was internationally known for its radio broadcasting, but also ran two hospitals. We would be assigned to the small jungle hospital located in the tiny village of Shell Mera. The village stood at the gateway to the vast jungle that spread westward across the entire South American continent. The village was infamous. Nine years earlier five missionaries stationed there had been murdered by the Waodani Indians deep in the jungle. The rest of the world knew them as the Auca Indians.

Were we ready to "give up everything we had" to be His disciples. Together in prayer, Joan and I agreed that we were ready to go. In early March 1965, we packed our bags and with our six month old infant daughter, Christy, flew to the rainforest of Ecuador.

What are you willing to give up to be a disciple of Jesus Christ? Little, or everything required?

MOUNTAIN DESCENT

*"Even though I walk through the valley
of the shadow of death, I will fear no evil,
for you are with me; your rod
and your staff, they comfort me."*

PSALM 23:4

The trip from Quito to Shell Mera was one that neither my wife or I will ever forget. Quito lies in the mountains at 10,000 feet with the jungle some 3000 feet below. No mission planes were available so we were driven there in a World War II jeep. It was open on three sides with a canvas top. The road was narrow and paved for the first twenty miles. Then we began our descent on an even more narrow, unpaved one-track road.

Passing through a gap in the mountains, a wide deep valley appeared before us. The dirt road curved along one side of the valley. It ran along the edge of a precipice with a sheer 1000-foot drop to the valley floor below. There were no guardrails or fences. At times the outside tires of the jeep tracked within inches of the precipice. In the passenger seat, I could look straight down to the distant valley floor. Alarmingly, numerous small memorials of flowers and crosses were scattered along the roadside. Each marked the deaths of those who missed the turns and plunged over the side.

We were also concerned that many of the curves on the road were blind and that traffic was traveling both ways along the precipice. As we rounded yet another blind curve, we noticed a large yellow bus lumbering up the grade toward us. It was overflowing with passengers and cargo. On its roof an assortment of sacks, packages, stalks of bananas, and even a few passengers rode precariously. Because of the width of the bus, those seated by the outside windows were actually suspended above the abyss. I glanced at my wife sitting in the back seat. She tightly held on to our infant daughter. The concern in both of our eyes was unvoiced, but obvious. "Even though I walk (ride) through the valley of the shadow death, I will fear no evil."

Suddenly our driver came to a stop. "What are we going to do now," I asked? "One of us has to back up until we find a space big enough for us to pass," he calmly replied. "You can be sure the bus won't back up," he added. He shifted the jeep into reverse and began carefully backing the jeep up the mountainside. Slowly we backed around the last blind curve. It was not like backing out of your driveway. Thankfully, no one was on the descent behind us. Within a quarter-mile, there was a slight widening of the road. There the jeep clung to the mountainside as the bus crept carefully around us. I selfishly was thankful that we were on the inside. As the rear of the bus cleared the jeep, several passengers, hanging onto the rear of the bus, waved a greeting. We thanked God for our safety.

What valleys are you walking through? To whom or what are you looking for safety?

DEPENDENCE

"I will lie down and sleep in peace, for you alone,
Lord, make me dwell in safety."

PSALM 4:8

After our arrived in Shell Mera, we were brought to the small hut that would be our home for the next three months. It was very small. There were only two rooms and a tiny bathroom. It had served as a bunkhouse for Shell Oil Company workers as they searched for oil. It was elevated two feet off the ground to discourage snakes as well as to create a buffer between the floor and the moist earth.

We were now in the rainforest of Ecuador with an average rainfall of 230 inches per year. We were told that the generator at the hospital would run a few hours each morning and evening. This would give us an opportunity to use the few electrical appliances we had. It would also light a bulb near the floor of our closet. The bulb was not to be turned off. Hopefully, its heat would keep our clothes and shoes from turning green. In the high humidity, mold appeared over night. The bulb was only marginally successful.

We returned to our hut after supper hoping to unpack before the lights went out. As we turned on the light switch, we saw movement along the walls of our home. Between the two-inch slats that covered the walls and ceiling we saw the long antennae of countless large jungle cockroaches. When the lights were turned off, the roaches would reappear, all six inches of them. But at least they disappeared when the lights came on. Looking more carefully around our home, we noted a peculiarity in the floor near the kitchen table. There was a round two-inch hole through which the ground could be seen with a flashlight. We learned the next morning that this was where Joan could sweep the bat dung that filtered down from our ceiling each day. Several hundred bats were sharing our home with us. Perhaps this was why Joan's mother had wanted us to leave the baby with her.

The flickering of the lights warned us they would soon be turned off for the night. We quickly lit a kerosene lantern before a night black as pitch settled around us. The air was soon filled with a cacophony of strange sounds as the nocturnal jungle creatures awakened. A few sounds, like those of the monkeys, were familiar but other sounds were frightening as the large jungle cats greeted the night.

Evening devotions took on a new intensity as the full realization of our total dependence on God flooded over us. There was so little here that we could control as our dangerous descent through the mountains reminded us. In reality, dependence on God is a daily need wherever we are. However, our dependence is inversely proportional to our mistaken notions of what we control. Total dependence on God is 24/7 yet we often live as if it is situational. "In peace I will lie down and sleep, for you alone, Lord, make me dwell in safety." (Psalm 4:8) Baby Christy was already asleep.

On what or whom do you depend? Yourself? The police? The locks on the door?

DECEPTION

*"The Lord saw how great man's wickedness
on the earth had become, and that every
inclination of the thoughts of the human
heart was only evil all the time."*

GENESIS 6:5

J oan and I soon settled in to a daily routine in Shell Mera. Joan took care of the baby, our small home, and prepared our daily meals. I worked in the outpatient clinic at the hospital and began taking a turn in obstetrics attending to nighttime deliveries. It was heady stuff for a medical student awaiting graduation. I was practicing medicine.

Two problems seen at the jungle hospital were unique in my limited medical experience.

I had not previously encountered charlatans or medical quacks at the University Hospital or in my several externships. I soon learned that those who deceive others for profit are not limited by nationality or culture. They are everywhere, even in the remote rain forests of Ecuador. A common ruse was to sell one of the Indians a vial of calcium carbonate and to tell them it was a medicine of great power. This was a cure for nearly every malady. As the charlatans rarely had needles or syringes, the jungle Indians frequently came to the hospital with a vial of the drug asking for an injection. When injected, the drug gives a warm flush beginning at the site of injection and then spreads rapidly throughout the body. It was very hard to convince the Indians that they had been cheated out of their money for each had felt the warm power surge through their bodies.

The second scam was more serious and was called phantom surgery. In this scam a superficial incision was made in the skin. The charlatan then presented the patient with a foreign object he had hidden in his hand. It was covered in blood and the patient was told this is what had caused the problem. The superficial incision was then closed with sutures. The danger was that the superficial incisions were frequently made at the sites where an appendix or gall bladder might be removed. If the patient later developed a real disease, surgery might be delayed, as the incision appeared to indicate the organ had been removed.

How easy it is for all of us to deceive others rather than speaking the truth. Total depravity, even in the unmapped rainforest, was clearly evident. Lying and deception indicate our hatred of others. It is the direct opposite of the summary of the law that commands us to love God above all and our neighbors as ourself.

Is speaking the truth difficult for you? Is speaking the truth situational when lying is more convenient or beneficial?

Jungle Trek

Full canoe (dugout)

BAD JUDGEMENT

"The lips of the righteous nourish many,
but fools die for lack of judgement."

PROVERBS 10:21

D r. Wally Swanson, a long time medical missionary in Ecuador, wrote a short story while in high school about bringing medical care to the jungle Indians of Ecuador. The story involved a dugout canoe trip deep into the jungle following the Napo River, one of the headwaters of the Amazon. He had long planned the trip but now was unable to go because of his wife's pregnancy and previous obstetrical complications. I was asked to take his place.

I flew first to the jungle mission station where another missionary had offered to be the river guide. Early the next morning, he and I began the long trek to the river. Bill warned me that it would be muddy and wet. That was an understatement. The rainforest receives nineteen feet of rain each year. Its tall, 200-foot, trees form a green canopy over the jungle floor. Although the sun was hot and bright, it did little to dry out the ground under the trees.

We sloshed along the muddy ground slipping and sliding. Before long each of us was covered with mud. Late that afternoon, we arrived at a small village on the Napo River. As we came out of the jungle, we presented quite a sight covered from head to toe with mud. Each of us carried bundles of clothing and medicine wrapped in plastic. Bill also had his carefully wrapped shotgun. Each of us wore a pith helmet. We took several pictures of each other, which to this day remain amusing. Hot and dirty, Bill suggested this would be a good place to swim, clothes and all.

I dove in first and was immediately surprised by the swiftness of the current. It rapidly carried me downstream and away from Bill. It was with great effort that I made it back to where I had plunged into the river. I had always considered myself to be a pretty good swimmer, but this frightened me. "Look before you leap" is a wise adage. An appropriate jungle corollary might be, check the current before plunging.

My judgment was poor and my actions foolish. My life was spared, this time. How is your judgment? Do you choose friends and lifestyle wisely? Do you daily seek a closer relationship with God? "...fools die for lack of judgement..." Proverbs 10:21

HOSPITALITY TO STRANGERS

*"For I was hungry and you gave me something
to eat, I was thirsty and you gave me something to
drink, I was a stranger and you invited me in."*

MATTHEW 25:35

Near the village a large number of Indian women were standing along the riverbank. Bill and I stood near a group that had gathered in a circle a few feet from the river. They talked and laughed together while chewing a squash-like fruit from one of the palm trees. Bill told me the fruit came from the Chonta palm and that wood from that tree was also used to fashion spears, bows, and arrows.

As the women socialized, they would intermittently spit out some of the chewed fruit onto an ever growing pile in the middle of their circle. When it reached a certain size, one of the women would carefully wrap it in banana leaves. Wrapped in its leafy cocoon, the chewed fruit would gradually ferment from their saliva. To welcome guests into their homes and villages, the women would first get a bucket of water from the river. They would then stir in a few handfuls of the fruit they had chewed a week or more before. The drink was called Chi-cha. Refusing it would be an insult to the hostess.

Feeling a light tap on my arm, I turned to see a smiling Quechua woman. She was holding a pint-sized tin bowl of Chi-cha. She held it out and offered it to me. The liquid resembled orange Kool-Aid and was cool and pleasant to the taste. I was very thirsty from our long trek and drank all of it. In truth I enjoyed it, that is, until early the following morning. That day Bill and I were to begin our three day trip in the dugout canoe. However, before leaving, I was forced to make several quick trips into the bush. The thought passed through my mind that Chi-cha was a viable competitor to Exlax. Rummaging through my medical bag, I found a small bottle of Kaopectate and promptly drank its contents. I could only imagine my embarrassment if the symptoms were to recur, while in the middle of the river, sitting among a dugout canoe full of people. I offered a short prayer and God was kind. The symptoms did not return.

Hospitality to strangers is a trait listed by Jesus as worthy of heavenly reward. While the results for me were not desirable, the custom and intent of their hearts was what God desired. In our modern cultures, we have often lost the art of hospitality to strangers. There are still many opportunities. Do you ever bring visitors home from church for a cup of coffee or a meal? Do you ever assist at the local food pantries and kitchens? Do you ever visit those in nursing homes, hospitals, or prisons?

RIVER TRIP

*"If I rise on the wings of the dawn, if I settle on
the far side of the sea, even there your hand will
guide me, your right hand will hold me fast."*

PSALM 139:9-10

Early the next morning, Bill and I joined six Quechua
Indians who frequently traveled the river. After intro-
ductions, we settled into their 20-foot dugout canoe. It would
be our transportation deep into the jungle. The Indians pushed
the canoe off the sandy bank and one of the men, holding a
long pole, took his place on the small rear platform.

After several hours on the river, he left his place on the
platform and knelt behind me in the canoe. One could feel the
increased tension as the Indians in the canoe chatted excitedly
and pointed upriver. The river had become noticeably rougher
and water was now splashing over the sides of the dugout.
Already the watertight ammunition box, in which I kept
my camera, was floating about my feet on the bottom of the
canoe. The 20-foot canoe, with its eight passengers, was rapidly
approaching a large whirlpool. It had formed where the river
made a sharp 75 degree turn to the west. To our left was a sheer

110-foot cliff whose grayish-white wall, from our position on the river, appeared to be directly in front of us. On the right, dense rainforest climbed abruptly uphill and directly in front of us was the whirlpool. Years earlier, we had been told, eight men from the Shell Oil Company lost their lives here.

The origin of the whirlpool, according to an old Indian legend, was that it was formed in the distant past during the time of their Inca forefathers. According to the legend, a long rope bridge woven from vines spanned the river from cliff top to forest. One day the Inca's trapped a large tiger on the bridge. Desperate for escape, it leaped from the bridge into the river below. Finally, exhausted from swimming, it sank to the bottom of the river. There it continued running in tight circles creating the whirlpool we now approached.

I hastily snapped a few pictures, grabbed the ammunition box, stuffed my camera inside, and secured the lid. The Indian nearest me handed me a paddle. I grasped the paddle tightly pulling hard on the right side of the canoe along with the others. The tall face of the cliff now towered above us as we strained hard against the paddles. Then just to the right, six or eight feet away, the vortex of the whirlpool appeared. The turbulent water swirled violently in a counter-clockwise direction resembling the funnel of a mid-western tornado. We skimmed along the edge of its turbulent spiral and briefly the canoe seemed to hesitate. Suddenly, as if fired from a slingshot, we rapidly accelerated into the turn of the river. Quickly I retrieved my camera, but it was already too late for pictures.

Rest assured, that wherever you are taken by circumstances or life, you are never beyond God's concern and care. He can and will guide you and care for you anywhere.

AUCA COUNTRY

You have heard that it was said to the people long
ago, 'You shall not murder, and anyone
who murders will be subject to judgment.'
But I tell you that anyone who is angry with his
brother will be subject to judgment...

"MATTHEW 5:21

The river was wider but our danger had now increased. The Quechua Indian at the rear of the canoe was careful to keep the dugout near midstream. We did not wish to be surprised by a sudden attack from the dense jungle. No danger was visible, but we had now passed an invisible boundary marking the Auca's country. A few Auca's were now Christians, but members of this tribe had murdered five missionaries eight years earlier. Violence was still a way of life for most. Sitting in the dugout we were clearly visible to anyone hiding in the dense jungle along the river's edge. They, on the other hand, were completely invisible to us.

The afternoon passed uneventfully and our passage downriver was smooth. At dusk we reached a small clearing on the opposite side of the river. Here we would spend the night.

Two small thatched buildings stood at its center. They were home to a Quechua Indian and his family. He was a Christian who was actively engaged in teaching and evangelizing others in his tribe.

After breakfast the following day, many Indians gathered in the clearing to see the doctor. A few needed injections of penicillin while most required medication for worms. Roundworm infections were common, especially among the children. The eggs of the worms are picked up from the soil and, because of the lack of soap or frequent hand washing, ingested. Untreated, they can cause pneumonia, weight loss, and even intestinal obstruction and death.

There were also a variety of rashes as well as various aches and pains that were annoying but not serious. Around noon, a young boy about fourteen years old was brought to the clinic. He had a jagged, dirty, festering wound on his right forearm. He and his brother had been attacked by a band of Auca Indians the day before. His brother had been killed. He escaped by running and hiding in the jungle. The wound was from a spear.

Under local anesthetic the wound was cleaned and debrided. He was then given tetanus immunization and a long acting penicillin injection. A clean dressing was applied and instructions given to his mother. Soon we were back on the river once again.

Few of us, I pray, will ever be involved in the taking of another human's life. Yet all of us at one time or another will be angry with a brother or a sister. Anger, Jesus said, is also a reason for judgment. Anger shows our lack of forgiveness for another. He who does not forgive cannot be forgiven.

A TASTE OF HEAVEN

*"After this I looked, and there before me was a great
multitude that no one could count, from every nation, tribe, people and language, standing before the
throne and before the Lamb..."*

REVELATION 7:9

We spent the weekend at a small mission station deep
in the jungle. Bill knew the pastor and his family. He
had also informed them that we were coming. They warmly
welcomed us into their home. It was a special weekend for it
was the annual gathering of the Christian Indians scattered
throughout the jungle. Hundreds had come for the fellowship
and special services, but most were there to witness the
baptism of fifty or more fellow Indians.

Following breakfast on Sunday morning, we all attended
the morning worship service. Although I could not speak the
Quechua dialect, during the singing of familiar hymns, my
English blended without difficulty with the Quechua language
surrounding me. After the service, we all began walking toward
the river for a baptismal service. I will never forget the sight.
On both sides of the river, many Indians were lining the tall
banks each dressed in white.

I stood in the water with my camera, as the new Christians one by one scrambled down the tall banks. Each waited his or her turn to wade to the pastor standing midstream. As each was baptized the pastor's voice rang clearly through the jungle, "I baptize you in the nambre of the Patre, est Hijo, et est Spiritu Sanctu." As I watched each head reappear from the water a Scripture verse rang in my head. "After this I looked, and there before me was a great multitude that no one could count, from every nation, tribe, people and language, standing before the throne and before the Lamb…" Revelation 7:9

The jungle Indians were but a portion of the Holy Catholic Church of our Apostolic confession. Do you recognize the Holy Catholic Church as it worships around the world each Sunday? Do you pray for them? The children's Sunday school song says it best. "Jesus loves the little children, all the children of the world. Red and yellow, black and white, they are precious in His sight!"

Quechua Indian Spiritual Conference

Headhunters near aircraft

Quechua Indian hunters

DO YOU SEE WHAT I SEE

"Sing for joy, O heavens, for the Lord has done this;
shout aloud, you earth beneath.
Burst into song, you mountains, you forests
and all your trees, for the Lord has redeemed
Jacob, he displays his glory in Israel."

ISAIAH 44:23

The flight began with a loud knock on our door early one morning. I opened the door and saw Dave Osterhuis, our missionary pilot, standing there. "You want to fly over the volcano?", he asked. I glanced over his shoulders and saw the Andes Mountains vivid against an azure sky. "I have not seen a cloudless sky like this in over two years," he added.

Within thirty minutes Joan and I joined Dave in the small Cessna 185. Christy hardly noticed our leaving as she began playing with the Osterhuis's children. Within ten minutes the towering volcano known as Sangay completely filled the view through the plane's windshield. Dave skillfully circled its 18,000-foot peak clockwise and then counterclockwise as all of us eagerly took pictures. Its sides were steep and barren and its summit snowcapped to within 50 feet of the cone at its peak. The cone was nearly perfectly round and grayish-black smoke ascended high into the sky above us.

Soon, we all developed headaches from the lack of oxygen so Dave lowered the plane to a more comfortable altitude. We flew north along the Andes range. Directly ahead of us was the most beautiful mountain I have ever seen. It was majestic seen from our home twenty miles away, but absolutely stunning as the aircraft climbed again to view its summit. This mountain is the remains of a long dormant volcano known as El Tar. The remnants of this mountain were as high as the cone of the volcano we had just visited. The peak of El Tar had been lost hundreds of years earlier in a violent explosion.

If the cone was replaced, geologists had speculated, the mountain would be nearly 40,000 feet high. The jagged remains were covered with ice and snow. In the center of the caldera, was a pristine lake that reflected the blue of the sky above as well as the ice and snow on the jagged peaks around it.

Dave said the Incas' had called this "Almighty mountain." The Spanish, when they arrived, viewed it as a great cathedral. Its jagged, flattened top appeared from below to be an altar. Hence it's Spanish name, El Tar. (the altar)

"...burst into song you mountains!..." (Isaiah 49:13) The Bible in many places says creation sings and speaks of its creator God. Do you see what I see? As you look at the creation around you, do you see its creator or only an accident of a violent explosion of gases eons ago?

HOPELESS

"May the God of hope fill you with all joy and peace
as you trust in him, so that you may overflow with
hope by the power of the Holy Spirit."

ROMANS 15:13

I was working in the outpatient clinic when I heard a
disturbance outside. Suddenly the door burst open and a
young Quechua man, accompanied by his friend, stumbled
into the clinic. He had lost hope and had attempted to take
his life that morning. His speech was unintelligible. He had
shot himself below the chin and the bullet passed through
his tongue finally lodging in the sinus below his left eye.
His tongue was grossly swollen, nearly filling the entire oral
cavity, and partially obstructing his breathing. Preserving his
breathing was our main concern as we had no ventilatory
equipment at the hospital.

We soon decided that flying the patient to the hospital
at Quito was our best option. The patient had never been in
a plane and refused to fly in it without his friend. The pilot
would not fly without medical supervision and the weight of
four people was more than the mission plane could lift over
the mountains. Providentially, a slightly larger plane from

another mission organization was on the runway at Shell Mera. After a few radio messages, it was released to us for the emergency flight.

The flight by air up the valley toward Quito was nearly as exciting as the trip down by jeep had been. We flew, twisting and turning, at 16,000 feet between the mountains. There was little communication with our patient as neither the pilot nor I spoke the Indian dialect. Neither Indian had previously flown and now they were soaring like birds. The mountainsides were often less than 100 feet from the wing tips with the peaks intermittently at eye level. Our patient had no major problems. His breathing, though noisy and labored, did not seem to worsen and his dressings controlled the bleeding.

As we neared our destination, a mountain wall rose across the valley separating us from Quito. The pilot flew parallel to the wall attempting to gain more altitude. But even this aircraft, with broader wings and a more powerful engine, could not gain altitude in the rarefied air. The weight of the four adults was a heavy load. "What can you do?", I asked. "We will continue to fly parallel and pray for a strong updraft to carry us up and over the top," the pilot replied. Within a few minutes a brisk updraft lifted us like an unseen hand. Quickly the pilot pushed the aircraft's nose toward the city below. We cleared the peaks with a close view of the buildings and the ground beneath. For a moment I thought we might shake hands with the occupants in the dome of a radar station. Soon we landed safely on the runway at Quito where an ambulance awaited us.

The patient's surgical problem was corrected the following morning and the bullet removed. His depression would take far longer. Hopefully, we could point him to the God of all hope. Do you feel hopeless? Do you know the One who can fill you with all joy and peace?

HEADHUNTERS

"You have heard that it was said, 'Love your neighbor and hate your enemy.' But I tell you, love your enemies and pray for those who persecute you, that you may be sons of your Father in heaven..."

MATTHEW 5:43-45

The Jivaro Indians are feared because of their reputation for headhunting. The severed head of a victim is considered a trophy of victory over their enemies. Headhunting has an ancient history. We read in the Old Testament of David cutting off the head of Goliath and the Philistines cutting off the head of King Saul. Even then, the severed head was a symbol of victory over their enemies.

The Jivaro Indians took it one step further by preserving the severed heads by shrinking them. After the victim's head was removed with a machete, the soft tissues of the scalp were skillfully removed from the boney skull. The lips, eyes, and nostrils were then sewn shut and a special mixture of sand and herbs were packed into this human tissue bag. Over a period of days, the tissues shrunk leaving a miniature, recognizable replica of the victim's head and face. The hair, unaffected by the process, now hung in long bangs from the scalp of the trophy.

I treated a survivor of one of those raids at the mission hospital. She was a young female who had been wounded by a homemade shotgun blast to her right shoulder and chest. While she had escaped with her life, her relative had not been as fortunate. Missionaries working with other bands of Jivaro Indians convinced the perpetrators to bury the head with the body.

Sadly, many of the victims were members of the same tribe, even relatives on whom they sought revenge for some real or imagined wrong. How horrible we would say.

Readers of this book would not consider killing their enemies or taking their heads. How many of us, however, have felt hatred for someone who has wronged us, even a relative? How many have thought or said, "I wish you were dead?" Jesus said, "Love your enemies." Not only must you not hate them, you must love them. Not only must you love them, you must pray for them. Do you or can you pray for the well-being of those who have sinned against you?

THE IMAGE of GOD

"So God created man in his own image,
in the image of God he created him;
male and female he created them."

GENESIS 1:27

A new runway had just been completed deep in the jungle in a Jivaro village. Dave, our missionary pilot, asked me to accompany him and hold a medical clinic. He felt it was an excellent opportunity to foster trust with the members of this village.

The plane flew 100 feet above the jungle. As far as we could see, a dense canopy of trees was broken only by the sporadic rocky peaks of a few hills. Below us flowed a tan-colored muddy river that wound back and forth upon itself like a serpent. Suddenly Dave grabbed my arm and pointed in the distance. Then I saw it, a small clearing surrounded by dense jungle. As we neared the clearing, I caught glimpses of the huts of the Jivaro's scattered among the trees. Small figures on the ground were looking up and waving, while even smaller figures were running toward the clearing.

Dave made a low level pass to check the runway for obstacles before safely dropping the aircraft onto the runway. The open-sided huts of several Indian families were now clearly visible. Small fires in front of each hut sent wisps of smoke ascending up through the trees. The Indians, who at first were clustered along the sides of the runway, now quickly surrounded the aircraft. Like children, they touched the wings of the "bird" that carried people. As we emerged from the plane, the bravest touched our clothing and even the skin of the pale creatures.

Headhunters, the name alone invokes fear, yet before me, and around me, stood dozens of broadly smiling men, women, and children. They were all curious, but some, especially the women, dared steal only shy glances. Their skin was bronze. They had coal-black eyes, straight black hair and standing in their bare feet were short in stature. All in all, they were a pleasant appearing people.

Somehow, in my imagination, headhunters had to be tall and ferocious. These people looked a lot like neighbors anywhere. "So God created mankind in his own image, in the image of God he created them; male and female he created them." (Genesis 1:27). Somehow the image of God is only completed by the vast diversity of the men and women He has chosen to create.

How do you feel about strangers, foreigners, those whose physical characteristics or languages are so different from your own? Do you think them strange, peculiar, or somehow less valuable to God than you are? Remember, God created them in His own image!

DO I SEE THE NEEDS OF OTHERS

*"If anyone has material possessions and sees
a brother in need but has no pity on him,
how can the love of God be in him?"*

1 JOHN 3:17

We flew into the jungle to bring medical care to those who had none. I was only the second white man that they had seen. They were curious, but seemed afraid of the stethoscope and otoscope that I carried in my hands. I decided to set up the clinic near the home of the local chief and make him my first patient.

I began by placing the stethoscope on my own chest and then let the chief look through the otoscope at my ear. The fear was quickly dispersed as I then placed the stethoscope on the chief's chest. I then placed an earpiece in each of his ears. As he listened to the loud beating of his own heart, his face broke into a wide grin. He then proudly verbalized his experience to his people. Now many wanted a turn and a half-hour soon passed, a half-hour punctuated by many smiles and peals of laughter. Now I could get down to making more serious evaluations.

The disease conditions prevalent among this remote group of people were not unexpected. There were many skin rashes as well as a variety of bacterial and fungal infections. Many adults were infected with worms, as were all the children. Heavy infestations can block the intestines causing death.

More frequently, in chronic infections, the worms are passed in their stools. Children often presented with severe coughing as they choked on the 8 to 12 inch worms or as the worms crawled out of their noses. We treated all with a bitter tasting but effective medication, Piperazine.

Some of the older individuals were chronically coughing and one of the older men presented with a right-sided pneumonia. I gave him an injection of penicillin and penicillin tablets. I hoped he would take them over the following week. He appeared well nourished, but in the back of my mind I worried about tuberculosis. TB could spread rapidly through this community because of its communal living arrangements. They also expectorated everywhere and whenever they felt the need. Without a doubt, basic education about sanitation, hand washing, and a better understanding of how diseases are spread would greatly benefit this community. This would come as the mission continued its contact with the Indians.

"If anyone has material possessions and sees a brother in need but has no pity on him, how can the love of God be in him?" (I John 3:17) One need not cross oceans or fly into remote jungles to find those with needs. Often those needs are present right next door or only a few miles from your home. How do you respond to the needs of others? Do you close your eyes, turn your head, or take a different route home? Do you think they should just work harder? Or do you first try to meet the immediate needs, if you are able, develop a relationship, and seek to direct and help them improve their situation?

SECURITY

"For he will command his angels concerning
you to guard you in all your ways; they will
lift you up in their hands, so that you will not strike
your foot against a stone."

PSALM 91:11-12

Dave taxied to the end of the runway as we prepared to leave our new Jivaro friends. Glancing down the runway, I knew this was the shortest strip I had ever flown off of.

It was 800 feet long with tall trees on all sides. As the trees had to be removed by hand, the Indians had not removed any extra trees once the runway was approved.

We accelerated down the runway and the trees at the far end loomed larger and larger. I almost felt I should wave my arms to give us extra lift. As we cleared the largest tree at the end of the runway, Dave casually remarked, "We probably ought to have them cut that tree down as well."

My admiration for the bush missionary pilots grew with each flight. Dave, along with numerous missionary pilots all over the world, flew in and over some of the most hostile and isolated places in the world. They flew day after day bringing missionaries, supplies, and medicine to those who had never had them. They ferried patients to hospitals where previously no help would have been available. They landed on cliffs, mountains, river banks, and in small jungle clearings.

Three christian military pilots conceived of the Missionary Aviation Fellowship, before the end of World War II. It's first flights began in 1946. Since that time they have been flying literally all over the world. When I flew with their pilots in the jungles of Ecuador, they had already flown for 19 years without an aviation fatality.

"He will give His angels charge over thee," the Psalmist says earlier, "if you dwell in the shelter of the most high" (Ps. 91:1) A testimony to the security God provides to those who love Him.

If we love God, it does not mean that we can do foolish things and expect His protection. It does mean that we can give up everything and risk everything to be His disciples. Our lives are secure and whatever happens, they are in the hands and will of a loving, faithful heavenly Father.

FLYING SNAKE

"Their venom is like the venom of a snake,
like that of a cobra that has stopped its ears,"

PSALM 58:4

We met them in the jungle at dusk. Rachael Saint and Dayauma, the first of the Auca Indian Christians, were trekking through the jungle. It was a pleasure and honor to meet these women. Much had been written about them after the deaths of five missionaries at the hands of the Auca's nine years earlier. One had been Rachael's brother, Nate.

We shared a dinner of roasted monkey around the fire that evening. After the meal I stepped back into the shadows cast by the trees. At my feet I thought I saw a leaf moving. I poked at the area with a stick. Suddenly, a large, moth-like creature flew up and landed on my right upper leg. It was a bit difficult distinguishing its features in the shadows. It appeared to have large brown wings and a long head shaped like a peanut. There were two red eyes, one on each side of the strange head.

I walked back toward the light of the fire to get a better look at it, while the creature continued to walk up and down my leg. Then one of the Indians squatting near the fire turned and looked at me. He jumped up and began shouting in Spanish, "Culabre Voladura, Culabre Voladura!" I caught the word for snake, but I didn't see one. I had never heard of a flying snake. He leaped toward me and with one swift motion of his hat swept the creature from my leg and to the ground. A large empty coffee can was quickly placed over it.

We poured a small amount of gasoline under the can and the creature quickly surrendered to the fumes. The brown wings were three inches in length and its head looked just like a green peanut with red eyes. Turning the creature over I saw the reason for its name. Between its rear legs was a large poisonous sac and a nearly one half-inch spear-like shaft it used to inject the poison. It probably would not have killed an adult, but would have been very painful and nauseating like a poisonous snake or scorpion bite.

The writer of the Psalm was not talking about poisonous snakes. He was making an analogy about what comes out of the mouth. What comes out of our mouths is often as poisonous as a snake's venom. The words can be very cruel and cause great harm.

What words come out of your mouth? Words of kindness and encouragement? Or words that bite and are deadly?

FALSELY ACCUSED

"But Paul said to the officers: "They beat us
publicly without a trial, even though we are
Roman citizens, and threw us into prison.
And now do they want to get rid of us quietly? No!
Let them come themselves and escort us out."

ACTS 16:37

A month before we left for Ecuador I had imported a single-lens Japanese camera. It was one of the best available at the time, but was illegal to import to the United States. I therefore shipped it to friends in Canada and paid Canadian import duties as I crossed back over the Ambassador Bridge.

As Christy, Joan, and I approached the custom officers on our return, we were struggling with two suitcases, a Jivaro blowgun, an Auca spear, and an Ecuadorian rug. There was also a box of gifts for those who had supported us. While fellow passengers raced through customs unheeded, two officers immediately confronted us. One spoke pleasantly with Joan and Christy while the other loudly and roughly ordered me to unpack everything and lay it on the floor. He continued to loudly and publicly berate me as various items were placed on the floor. Our welcome home was a public embarrassment.

His real concern was the Pentax camera hanging around my neck. He blatantly accused me of smuggling. He gave no credence to my story about Canadian import duties. As he continued to loudly accuse me, Christy began to cry. I felt hurt and angry. I searched in vain through my wallet for the Canadian customs receipt. I began to fear I had left it at home. The longer I searched the more I was berated.

The officers then switched places and the "good cop" spoke quietly with me. I laid all the contents of my wallet on a table, and when I thought it was empty, I saw the pink corner of the customs receipt. It was carefully tucked in a secret fold of the wallet. I thrust it at the officer and reinforced the point with a pointed, "I was not lying." He glanced at the receipt and patted me on the back. There was no apology but he carefully helped me pick up all the items scattered on the floor. He helped me repack them and then escorted us out of the customs area.

We were not thrown in prison, only threatened publicly. We were considered guilty without investigation. Have you ever been publicly humiliated by those in authority? Has your word been taken as worthless? It often seems harder to forgive those who trespass against us especially when they are also wrong. Even St. Paul wanted an apology. The Bible adds, " "They (magistrates) came to appease them and escorted them from prison..." (Acts 16:39) Irregardless, forgiveness is the Christian's answer.

Headhunter's chief

Baptism at Spiritual conference

RENDER UNTO CAESAR

"He said to them, Then give to Caesar
what is Caesar's and to God what is God's."

LUKE 20:25

The year 1965 saw a large mobilization of troops and supplies as America became more fully involved in the Vietnam War. I was, however, surprised to receive a letter from the United States Department of Defense. All of my fellow interns, and some of the residents, received one as well. It was brief and the bottom line was clear, "You may volunteer or be drafted."

There was a mixed opinion about how we should respond. Some of our non-medical peers were burning their draft cards and fleeing to Canada. No one at the hospital wished to do that. A few of the doctors volunteered, while the majority decided to wait and see whether they would be drafted after all.

My father, with two of his brothers and a sister, served in World War I. Two of my older brothers served in World War II and one of them lost his life as a medic. As I at this time had no plans for residency, I called the Department of Defense. "What is the benefit of volunteering?" I asked. "You may pick the service in which you wish to serve," was the prompt reply. I chose the air force and was given a commission as a first lieutenant. After completing my internship and several months of training at Aerospace School, I would receive an assignment and enter the service as a captain.

Little did I know that my Intern colleagues, who had not volunteered, would be joining me in San Antonio, Texas, the following year. All were drafted into the army. While I often rode in an air-conditioned bus to Aerospace School training, they were learning to crawl on the ground at Fort Sam Houston.

As a physician I had no problem in "rendering unto Caesar." Jesus said we must give Caesar what he is due. One of those responsibilities was military service. Others had different opinions about the war and refused to serve in any capacity.

KINDNESS

*"...and to godliness, brotherly kindness
and to brotherly kindness, love."*

2 PETER 1:7

Joan was nearing the end of her second pregnancy. She saw her obstetrician at the hospital, and although not yet in labor, was admitted. Her first delivery had been only an hour and the obstetrician did not want her to return home. I saw her briefly as she was taken to the delivery floor, but was extremely busy working a 24-hour shift in the emergency room.

In the emergency room, all of the rooms and beds were occupied and more patients were still in the waiting room. I had just about given up hope of finding time to see my second child born. There was so much work that I did not want to ask someone else to do it for me. Then the Senior OB resident, Dr. Joe Cook, appeared in the emergency room. "Harry, you belong upstairs with your wife, I will cover the emergency room for you until she delivers," he announced.

I thanked him profusely and raced upstairs to see my second child, son Tim, delivered. He weighed over nine pounds and once again his mother delivered in an hour. Tim was healthy and there were no complications. I kissed Joan and then raced back down the stairs to finish my shift in the ER.

Kindness is one of the virtues that the Apostle Peter listed as present in a well-rounded, fruitful Christian life. In the gospel of Matthew, when Jesus discussed the judgment, He blessed those who fed the hungry, gave water to the thirsty, clothed the naked, and looked after the sick as if they had done it to Him. Like Dr. Cook, they did not have to be asked, begged, or cajoled. Kind people see a need and fill it. It is as natural to them as breathing. God's love flows naturally from them to others.

Are you kind? Is it natural for you to show kindness or must you be begged or cajoled?

"And to godliness, brotherly kindness; and to brotherly kindness, love." 2 Peter 1:7

New U.S. Air Force Captain and Family

SACRIFICE

"No, I beat my body and make it my slave
so that after I have preached to others, I myself will
not be disqualified for the prize."

1 CORINTHIANS 9:27

Interns in 1965 literally belonged to the hospital. It was not servitude, but the next thing to it. We were expected to work eighty hours each week with most shifts twenty-four hours on and twenty-four hours off. For this we were remunerated at the princely sum of about 80 cents an hour. In addition, we could eat all our meals at the hospital while on duty and our families were allowed one meal each week. We, along with our families, were also provided lodging in the intern quarters.

There were no limits to the number of patients we could see in twenty-four hours. The number of patients was determined simply by the number of patients admitted to that hospital service. In those days of liberal health insurance, patients were routinely admitted the night before surgery for a workup. Medical patients were also frequently admitted for a more thorough testing when a diagnosis was obscure.

Laboratory testing and radiological services were primarily inpatient procedures not the outpatient procedures they later became. Added to all these patients, were those with severe illnesses, mothers in labor, and all those admitted through the emergency room. Each patient had to be seen and evaluated for hospital admission and followed while there.

It was up to the medical inpatient staff, interns, and residents to see that all the work was done. It was a grueling pace. We spent very little time with our wives and families, and when we were home, we were frequently exhausted. However, with the long hours and large numbers of patients, each new physician saw and handled a large variety of medical problems and diagnoses. The wide exposure to patients was fascinating and the sacrifice worthwhile to finish training and to legally become a physician. That was the prize.

The Apostle Paul stressed how an athlete sacrifices his body in training for races or boxing; sacrifices so that he will win and receive the prize. These sporting events were an analogy of the Christian life. Are you willing to sacrifice, to be a living sacrifice for Christ? Are you literally willing to beat your body to avoid the temptations of sin? Like Paul, will you strive for the prize?

PREPARATION

*"Proclaim this among the nations: Prepare for war!
Rouse the warriors! Let all the fighting men draw
near and attack. Beat your plowshares into swords
and your pruning hooks into spears..."*

JOEL 3:9-10

I arrived in San Antonio in mid-July 1966 to begin my basic and specialized training in aerospace medicine. The classes were stimulating so it was not difficult to return to school. As flight surgeons, we would be responsible for overseeing the health of the flight crews. The purpose of the school was to teach us about the particular medical problems and dangers associated with flight.

Our basic training was routine except that all members were physicians. There was a special emphasis on parachute jumping and the use of ejection seats. For the most part this was fun, at least I enjoyed it. We were not required to make an actual jump. We were, however, trained in landing. They trained us by suspending us twenty feet off the ground and then without warning dropped us from the parachute harnesses. We were taught to roll forward with the impact to absorb the shock of landing.

A second danger was that after hitting the ground the open chute could be dragged by a strong wind. Many parachutists have been severely injured or killed as the wind dragged them over fences, barb wire, and other obstacles. In landings at sea, some had drowned as the wind-billowed chute dragged them underwater. They trained us for this by dragging us behind a tractor along the ground. The tractor continued to drag us until we mastered the quick release device on the harness strap. Some had a long ride.

Ejection seats were more fun, like a carnival ride. The ejection seat, taken from an aircraft, sat on the ground and was attached to a vertical track extending more than fifty feet into the air. It was armed with a 55-millimeter artillery shell just like those in the aircraft. When the shell exploded, the seat was rapidly ejected to the top of the vertical track.

It was not all fun and games. We were shown the autopsy slides of airmen who had ejected into thunderstorms and whose bodies now appeared to be shot with buckshot. We saw the x-rays of a pilot, who attempting to make his seat more comfortable, put a foam cushion beneath him. His body now rested on the cushion and was not pressed against the seat. On ejection, the seat compressed the foam cushion traveling a short distance before reaching his body. The impact between seat and body fractured two of his vertebra. Finally, a slow-motion film of an ejection showed the seat revolving 50-60 revolutions per minute as it hit the airstream around the plane. If one were not tightly gripping the armrests, one's arms would be ripped out of their sockets.

Prepare for war! The prophet Joel was writing about the time of the last judgment. The Vietnam War was but one in a nearly continuous history of man's wars. Peace, peace but there will be no peace until the Prince of Peace enters every heart. Pray for that time!

A HOME

"Cast your cares on the Lord and he will sustain you..."

PSALM 55:22

My military assignment was to Andrews Air Force base in Washington, D.C. We arrived on a Friday morning. It was extremely hot, and our old Pontiac lacked air conditioning. I reported to the flight surgeons' office and met my commanding officer. One of our first needs was a home, and I asked about housing. Base housing? The colonel was amused by my request. "We don't have base housing for captains here. You will have to find your own, off-base. I will give you the name of a realtor," he added. "Now, until you find housing, the motel across the street can house your family. I will expect you to report for duty at 8:00 a.m. Monday morning." We saluted, and I was dismissed.

I returned to a sizzling car to find a wife and two very hot children. We drove to the motel and registered for three nights. After cooling off in the air-conditioned room, we met with the realtor. And so began a fruitless search for housing. An old house in the country met our budget, but was otherwise unacceptable. Similarly, apartments for rent were all over $400 a month, on upper floors, or in terrible neighborhoods. It was already four o'clock. Joan and I were now thoroughly discouraged. I took Joan and the children back to the motel to rest.

Discouraged, I sat for a moment in the motel parking lot and offered up a short prayer. "Lord, things are not working out the way we planned. We still need a place to live. Show me where to go." I turned onto Suitland Drive, the main road leading away from the base. I had driven only a mile when I saw the new four-story apartment complex, Regency Park. It was very attractive, with a large swimming pool in the middle of the complex. I was sure it was too expensive. I entered the manager's office. "Are there any apartments left for rent?" I asked. She paused and I dreaded her reply.

"Yes, we have one two-bedroom apartment left," she responded with a smile. "If you like, I will show it to you." I followed her down a flight of stairs to a ground level apartment. It had never been occupied. From the kitchen, sliding doors opened to a large grassy area on a dead end street behind the complex. I was afraid to ask the cost. "It is $299 a month," she said. I could hardly believe my ears. "I know we will take it, but I would like to bring my wife back here first," I replied. "Please don't rent it to someone else!" She smiled broadly at my exuberance. "Don't worry; I will hold it for you."

I thanked God all the way back to the motel. There, I awoke my sleepy wife and children who were not as excited as I, until they saw it. The rent and deposit emptied our checking account.

"Cast your cares on the Lord..." (Psalm 55:22) How often God is the last resort after we have exhausted our plans, the realtor or anyone else we sought to meet our needs. Why are we so slow to lean on whom we should depend?

TOMORROW

*"Therefore do not worry about tomorrow,
for tomorrow will worry about itself.
Each day has enough trouble of its own."*

MATTHEW 6:34

My meager pay when an intern, along with Joan's part-time work at the hospital, had barely kept us afloat. We had meager possessions, little savings, and a school debt. Our family had grown to four. We naively left Grand Rapids with $125 in our pockets. No one had yet conceived of credit cards or maybe we just had never heard of them. We expected to reach Washington after spending one night in a motel. Expecting base housing, we hoped to have enough money left for expenses, mostly groceries, until my next paycheck in two weeks.

We were now facing a motel bill for three more nights at $22.50 a night. We had just emptied our checking account to secure housing. We had $78 and change for our motel bill and food for the next two weeks. We ate our meals in the motel room splitting sandwiches and rolls during our stay there. We did splurge one day at the new McDonald's near the base. The hamburgers were only 25 cents apiece.

Monday morning we prepared to check out of the motel. I now had only $70 counting my change. As I prepared to give the clerk $67.50 he asked, "Do you have orders to report to the base Captain?" "Yes sir, I do," I replied. Reaching into an inside pocket I handed him my orders. "Then it is $33.75 that you owe me Captain. Military with orders get their rooms for half price," he added with a smile.

We dropped the U-Haul on the dead end street near our new apartment. Joan would spend the day with the children moving our few belongings into the empty rooms. We would be sleeping on the floor, but we had a home and $33 to buy gas and groceries before my next paycheck.

Do you worry about tomorrow? Who doesn't worry about tomorrow? Those individuals who trust in the Lord. Lord, strengthen my faith!

Doctor in Flight Suit

LIGHT

*"In the same way, let your light shine before men,
that they may see your good deeds and praise
your Father in heaven."*

MATTHEW 5:16

I drove to the base and reported for duty. After a morning of orientation the colonel instructed me to take the afternoon off and to do some furniture shopping. We drove downtown and parked outside the store the Colonel had recommended. We glanced at the furniture in the windows and immediately felt like poor country cousins. Everything was elegant, but so expensive. A sofa and chair were $1400. We had hoped to spend little more than that for all our furniture, and we needed nearly everything. We politely listened and then thanked the Colonel's friend. "We would first like to do a bit more looking around," we said.

We found a furniture sale at Montgomery Ward with a credit plan. For less than $600, we purchased a lovely bedroom set with two dressers, a mirror, and a mattress. We often look back and smile at that purchase. The furniture was all wood in those days and that set lasted us 30 years. Others are still using some of it.

That evening we drove around the Suitland area. A few miles away we found a small family owned furniture store. There were many reasonably priced items to which we were attracted. Meeting the owner, I explained that we had no money and no furniture. I had recently been stationed at Andrews Air Force Base as a physician. If he would trust me, I would pay a portion of the bill every two weeks when I was paid. That night we purchased a sofa, a chair, and two end tables.

Three months later, I entered his store to make the final payment. The bookkeeper stated the final bill to be $35 dollars less than what I owed. I said this must be a mistake and went out to the car to get my receipt. When I returned the owner was standing behind his wife, the bookkeeper. I showed them my receipt and they saw the error she had entered into the books. As I paid the full amount, the owner looked at me and said, "Why would you do that? You could have walked out of here with $35." "I am a Christian," I replied. "That was your money, not mine. It would have been stealing." As I turned to leave the store, the owner exclaimed, "Captain, you can shop in my store anytime you want!"

"In the same way, let your light shine before men..." (Matthew 5:16) Witnessing can be, but is not necessarily, a Biblical exhortation. People commonly view the lives we live. Do we practice what we preach?

USE A LARGE MEASURE

"Give, and it will be given to you. A good measure,
pressed down, shaken together and running over,
will be poured into your lap. For with the measure
you use, it will be measured to you."

LUKE 6:38

Slowly over the first ten months in Washington, Joan and I were able to furnish the apartment. We had still not purchased a kitchen table. We had managed to get by with a card table we had received as a wedding present. It was not well suited for entertaining, but most of our friends remembered a similar situation. The main problem was the growing children. As they grew, it was obvious we needed something larger and sturdier.

We stopped again at the furniture store where we had made our earlier purchases. There we found a sturdy wooden kitchen set with six chairs. As we made the down payment, the owners' delivery truck pulled around to the rear of the store and it was quickly loaded. When we arrived home, the truck was waiting on the dead end street behind the apartment.

Six weeks later we made yet another stop at the store. We needed a pair of large table lamps for the end tables we had purchased eight months earlier. As the family entered the store the owner greeted us cheerfully. "What can I do for you, Captain?" he asked. "We need a pair of large table lamps," I replied. "Buy any lamp in the store and the second one is free," he answered with a smile. "Aw, you don't have to do that," I said. "I know," he replied, "but I want too. The second lamp is free."

"...For with the measure you use, it will be measured to you." (Luke 6:38) What measure do you use in your relationships with others and your family? In the verses prior to this one I, the writer, expand "measure" to include many of our relationships with others. He speaks of judging others, condemning others, and forgiving others. It really concerns "all" our relationships. Do you measure with a large overflowing barrel or a small tin cup?

Air Force One

ACCEPTED

"For the kingdom of God is not a matter of eating and drinking, but of righteousness, peace and joy in the Holy Spirit, because anyone who serves Christ in this way is pleasing to God and and approved by men."

ROMANS 14:17-18

One of the joys of being a flight surgeon was the requirement to have at least four hours of flying each month. This practical experience with flight crews helped us understand their special medical needs. I was to fly in all sorts of aircraft from fighter trainers, helicopters, small passenger planes, to large passenger jets.

Some flights were boring, like an hour or two of flying "touch and goes." These flights allowed pilots to practice repetitive take offs and landings. Other flights were fun and eagerly accepted. One of my favorite flights was accompanying instructor pilots while they tested aircraft after mandatory maintenance. All were tested before student pilots were allowed to fly them. The maneuvers would include maximum power take offs, aileron rolls, power climbs, tight turns, and flame out landings.

The T-3 trainer was a two-seat fighter trainer with a full glass canopy. It was a subsonic aircraft that could reach speeds of 600 miles per hour. To fly, one needed full-flight gear, which included a helmet with built-in communication, flight suit, parachute, and survival kit. Prior to take off, an aircraft mechanic ensured that each passenger was properly strapped into the ejection seat. He then checked the oxygen hose and finally removed the pin that armed the ejection seat.

The instructor pilots frequently took a perverse delight in seeing just how much the back seat passenger could take. It was part of the initiation that gained the doctor acceptance and approval from the flight crews. Certain maneuvers were worse than others. I could handle the aileron rolls and flying upside down for a while. Occasionally, my stomach would signal that it had enough. I did not want to cry "uncle," but the last thing I wanted to do was vomit in the aircraft. First of all there was no place to go with the vomit. Secondly, with all the flight gear, it would just be a colossal mess. Thirdly, I did not relish the embarrassment of sitting in the vomit until the flight ended. Finally, whoever vomited in the fighter had to clean it out!

While I never did vomit and did not cry "uncle," I certainly was nauseated at times. I learned to use my emergency oxygen supply whenever needed and tried to fix my eyes on the horizon outside the plane. I wanted to be accepted.

Paul said that it is by righteousness, peace, and joy in the Holy Spirit that we are accepted by God and man. We all want the acceptance of man, whether at home, work, or play. How many of us strive to live our lives so we will be acceptable to God?

TRUST AND OBEY

"Trust in the LORD with all your heart and lean not
on your own understanding; ⁶ in all your ways submit
to him, and he will make your paths straight."

PROVERBS 3:5-6

Late one afternoon I flew in a thunderstorm. The view
of the storm was incredible through the glass canopy
surrounding us. The rain pounded on the canopy as we flew
through the dark clouds, illuminated intermittently by flashes
of lightening. Buffeted by the winds, the fighter trainer rose
and fell as we accelerated through the storm. Once we left the
base, we did not see the ground again until we returned. We
were totally surrounded by dark, swirling clouds.

When the instructor had taught us about spatial
disorientation at aerospace school, it was only a concept. Now
it was real. Without the instruments, it was impossible to tell
whether we were flying level, climbing, circling, banking, or
upside down. Many have died in what is known as the death
spiral. Pilots without instruments or not trusting them, think
they are flying level, while all the time they are flying in a
spiral toward the ground and their death.

The pilot's voice echoed in my headset, "You want to take her back, Doc? The stick is yours. Just listen to the controller and watch your instruments. He will give you the headings back to the base." I grasped the stick between my legs. Amazing how the aircraft responded to the slightest movement. A voice commanded in my ears: "Flight 807, turn west ten degrees and descend to eight thousand feet." The controller, if he was watching the radar, might have thought we had an early happy hour. My first attempts were imprecise, but after a few more turns they improved. What a blast!

All too soon the pilot took full control once again. Changes in altitude and new headings were executed with precision. Suddenly, out of the darkness and storm, a glowing brightness increased beneath us. "You are on the glide path," the controller's voice assured us. We had flown for over two hours in wind, rain, and darkness. We had no visual confirmations of our position, only the voice in our ears that guided us precisely and surely back to base. A voice we had to trust and obey.

Flying in a thunderstorm is a lot like life. How often we are blinded by life's trials and do not know which way to turn. "...Lean not on your own understanding." (Proverbs 3:5) Unfortunately, that is where most lean and fail... The writer of the Proverbs said, "Trust in the Lord with all your heart... and in all your ways submit to him and he will make your paths straight." (Proverbs 3:5-6) You have to trust your heavenly father and obey Him to come safely home.

TROUBLE

"God is our refuge and strength, an ever present
help in trouble. ²Therefore we will not fear,
though the earth give way and the mountains
fall into the heart of the sea."

PSALM 46:1-2

I n 1968, Washington, D.C. did not escape the racial unrest
seething across the country. Salvation City, a collection of
cardboard and plastic shelters, surrounded the Memorial Pond
in front of the Lincoln Memorial. Thousands of dissatisfied
blacks from the city, along with protestors from all over America,
agitated there for a better life and equal opportunities.

In that volatile atmosphere, Joan and I were the dinner
guests in the home of a black master sergeant from my office.
Sergeant Berthea and his wife were a delightful couple. He and
I had hit it off immediately after my assignment to the base. He
had been in the air force for many years. We had many frank
and interesting discussions and had become good friends.

His wife prepared an excellent dinner, and after eating
we adjourned to the living room for coffee. In the midst of
our discussion, we heard the sounds of many sirens close by.

He immediately turned on his television set and we learned about the rioting and multiple house fires only a few blocks away. Several blocks of the city from 7th to 14th Street already were ablaze with many fires. We rapidly concluded that this was not an area where Joan and I should spend the evening. The sergeant offered to accompany us in his car, but we felt it unnecessary.

We thanked Mrs. Berthea for the lovely dinner and then gathered our coats and headed for the front door. The sergeant could not resist a good-natured parting shot as we opened the door. "Don't forget to keep your lights on, Honky." We all had a good laugh, although Joan and I were nervous about leaving the neighborhood. We did not know what to expect other than some here were very angry and violent.

Have you ever been afraid? Of course you have. Little children fear the darkness. Young people fear getting through school. Young families fear for their children. Older folks fear disease and cancer. Life is uncertain and often frightening. One thing is sure, "God is our refuge and strength, an EVER PRESENT help in trouble." Psalm 46:1

HONOR THE KING

"Show proper respect to everyone, love the family
of believers, fear God, honor the King..."

1 PETER 2:17

The presidential wing is stationed at Andrews Air Force Base in a securely guarded and separately fenced off area. It is here that Air Force One is stored and where the flight crews who attend the president and other high-ranking officials are stationed. I, along with several other flight surgeons, was cleared for presidential duty. The flight surgeon's duty was to cover presidential arrivals and departures from either a helicopter or an ambulance parked on the flight line.

The helicopter had to be in position thirty minutes before the arrival or departure of Air Force One. The physician was to be accompanied by two firemen in asbestos suits and a fire suppression kit was hung below the helicopter. If Air Force One crashed on takeoff or landing, our responsibility was to rescue the president and administer immediate medical aid. If he landed safely, our second responsibility was to follow his helicopter back to the White House. After the president exited the Marine One helicopter on the White House lawn, we were free to return to base.

We took turns covering the president from either the helicopter or from an ambulance that was stationed on the flight line. On the flight line, we were among numerous Secret Service agents who stood on the tarmac. If we left the ambulance, our presidential clearance badge was immediately examined. The agents closely guarded the president and his family as they walked to or from Air Force One. It was on these occasions that we had the opportunity to view the presidential party pretty closely. The security and efforts to protect his life were in honor of the position God had placed him.

"Honor the King." We honor the president because there is no authority that God has not established. That honor is irrespective of political or other disagreements with the individual. "Show respect to everyone" because they bear the image of God. "Love the brotherhood of believers" as they are your brothers and sisters in Christ. "Fear God, for it is the beginning of wisdom." Psalm 111:10

President Johnson exiting Marine I helicopter

TRUST

"Do not put your trust in princes, in mortal men,
who cannot save. When their spirit departs,
they return to the ground, on that very day
their plans come to nothing."

PSALM 146: 3-4

Flight surgeons assigned to the presidential wing, occasionally accompanied governmental officials on trips. We served as the medical officers on such flights. One Friday, I was assigned to accompany a group of congressmen flying to Guantanamo Bay, Cuba.

The flight began at Andrews Air force Base in Suitland, Maryland. Thirty-two congressmen boarded the flight at Andrews AFB, while three more joined us after we stopped at an air base in Florida. While this was booked as an "official trip", in realty it was just another weekend of fun and frolic in the Caribbean at the taxpayer's expense.

Many of the congressmen drank liberally on the flight to Cuba. Frankly, too many were inebriated. As we approached the island, several of the more inebriated members were still standing in the cockpit. As we were not permitted to invade Cuban air space, the landing at Guantanamo Bay was tricky. To land the pilot had to approach the airfield through the mountains.

As we neared the island, the pilot called me forward to the cockpit. He asked for my help in escorting these "gentlemen" back to their seats. He did not want to be distracted by inebriated passengers during this difficult landing. I was frankly disappointed as I shepherded the men out of the cockpit and back to their seats. One individual was particularly disappointing to me. He had been a teenage idol of mine because of certain athletic accomplishments. Now he too was inebriated. I expected more from the leaders of our country. These were the men who essentially made the laws and told the rest of us how to live, yet were unable to conduct themselves properly in public.

How often do we idolize those in positions of authority and power? In difficult situations we trust them to correct the problems and to save us. The Psalmist wrote, "Put not your trust in princes." Nothing has changed in the past two thousand years. "Princes" are still, "mortal men who cannot save." Honor them as representatives placed in authority by God, but trust only in God to save or deliver.

INTEGRITY

*"And David shepherded them with integrity of heart;
with skillful hands he led them."*

PSALM 78:72

One of my favorite trips occurred the day after the outbreak of the first Arab-Israeli war in 1967. I had been scheduled as the flight surgeon to accompany Secretary of State Dean Rusk. He was scheduled to visit Copenhagen and the Scandinavian countries. The sudden outbreak of war in the Middle East changed his plans. Instead of Scandinavia, he was forced to fly to an emergency meeting of NATO in Luxemburg. I was disappointed in not visiting the Scandinavian countries, but excited about traveling with the secretary of state.

As this was a state visit, we were given Air Force Two for the flight. It is called Air Force One only if the President is aboard. Security was tight for 1967, in that we were required to keep our personal luggage with us until it was taken aboard the aircraft. In light of today's security measures, it was a very simple precaution. The 60s was still a time of innocence despite the fact that a president had been assassinated four years earlier.

The secretary's wife accompanied him on the flight, along with his personal entourage that included many Secret Service agents. Both he and his wife were approachable and appeared more like a couple you might meet on Sunday at church. Although the flight was luxurious with beautiful flowers and White House china, both of them appeared to be without pretense.

Mr. Rusk served as secretary of state during the Bay of Pigs disaster, the Cuban missile crisis and the Vietnam War. He served two presidents. He was a man respected for his integrity even by those who disagreed with his policies. He conducted diplomacy in a quiet, unassuming way. It would be wonderful if all members of congress could conduct themselves with the same integrity. He was not a "respecter of persons." He was kind and courteous even to the lowest ranking airman. He was a Christian and his life reflected it.

Integrity today for many is a difficult concept. Some even say if a politician's lips are moving, he is lying. What can we believe from the news reports, the congressmen, the statements of politicians? What can be believed about the words that come out of our mouths? If we profess to be Christians, the words of our mouths and the actions of our lives will all have integrity.

DWELL IN SAFETY

"While people are saying, 'Peace and safety', destruction
will come on them suddenly, as labor pains on a
pregnant woman, and they will not escape."

1 THESSALONIANS 5:3

In the summer of 1967, two of my brothers and their families came to visit us. Bob and Jack were avid campers and had even constructed their own pop up campers. Between the two families, there were twelve individuals. We expected to feed everyone at our apartment, but were unable to sleep everyone there. Unfortunately, at that time there were no campgrounds in the Suitland, Maryland, area or near Washington, D.C.

I discussed the problem with a sergeant whose family lived in the base trailer park.

"No problem, Doc, there is a vacant area behind our trailers. It is just under the trees at the end of the main runway. We can easily park two campers there." "But how will we get them past the guards at the gate each night?" I asked. "I will talk with the guards and you should accompany them on the first trip," he replied. "It will work out just fine."

True to his word, the sergeant cleared the way for the brothers to set up camp behind the base trailer park. It was a beautiful spot with trees and a large grassy area. There was a unique downside. All types of aircraft, including fighters, helicopters, cargo and transport planes, and even Air Force One, flew over their heads at all hours of the day or night. I was carefully scrutinized whenever I was on the flight line prior to the take off of Air Force One. Yet here were two civilian families in pop-up campers. They slept there for over a week nearly in the shadow of Air Force One. President Kennedy had been assassinated only four years earlier. The campers had never been searched.

I am sure the Secret Service felt all was peace and safety at Andrews Air Force Base. Certainly, there was no danger from my brothers, but could others just as easily have gained access to the base with the Secret Service none the wiser?

The writer to the Thessalonians was not talking about protecting the president. He was talking about Christ coming as a thief in the night. Coming at a time when many individuals felt their lives were safe and secure. There was time; they could make their decision for Christ later. Don't wait, "…destruction may come on you as suddenly as labor pains on a pregnant woman…" I Thessalonians 5:3

ARMAGEDDON

*"...Blessed are those who are invited to the wedding
supper of the Lamb!..."*

REVELATION 19:9

In the 1950s and 60s there was a lot of talk about Armageddon, a nuclear holocaust which would destroy the earth and mankind as we knew it. People dug nuclear shelters in their backyards and school children drilled for a nuclear attack. A national warning system was put in place. Throughout the country air raid sirens were set up to give individuals thirty minutes to find shelter from the total destruction that awaited them.

That is also when Silver Dollar was born. It was a specialized wing of the air force whose responsibility was to protect the president in the event of a nuclear attack on Washington, D.C. The aircraft were jammed with the latest specialized communication gear. This would allow the president to continue the function of government even if Washington was destroyed. The planes, when airborne, were capable of contacting telephones worldwide. They were also known as Flying Command Posts. Three aircraft were kept at Andrews

AFB and three others in Colorado. One was always ready to fly at a moments notice.

The 707 aircraft were refitted during John F. Kennedy's presidency. Because of his severe, painful, back problems, each had a specially constructed chair in the command post. In 1967, I was told each chair cost $10,000.

Late in the year I was permitted to accompany one of the backup aircraft as a flight surgeon. We flew to Japan on a training mission to allow squadron members the opportunity to maintain their skills. I had a short stint in the "chair", but lacked sufficient rank to stay there very long. Those of us not assigned to the squadron did not have seats on the aircraft. They were reserved for those with specific functions. We slept lying on the bare fuselage.

The fear of a nuclear Armageddon has lessened considerably, but remains a remote possibility. Man has spent incredible amounts of money and effort to maintain life as we know it. There may not be an Armageddon, but all of us will die sometime. "…Blessed are those who are invited to the wedding supper of the Lamb…!" Revelation 19:9

WISE

*"Therefore everyone who hears these words of mine
and puts them into practice is like a wise man
who built his house on the rock."*

MATTHEW 7:24

Living in the nation's capital made our home a vacation destination for many family members and friends. Throughout the two years I was stationed at Andrews AFB, we chauffeured numerous friends and relatives to the various monuments, museums, and government buildings. I said we, but primarily this responsibility fell to my wife, Joan. On many occasions I was on duty and could not accompany them on the forays into the city. I am sure Joan was the chauffeur at least 80 percent of the time.

Our only means of transportation was an old, four-door 1961 Pontiac. It had a peculiar idiosyncrasy. Unpredictably, it would not start although the key was in the ignition. Several mechanics had examined the car and various electric parts such as the condenser, battery, and generator had been replaced. All was to no avail. The only thing that consistently worked was crossing the condenser and the generator with the metal portion of a screwdriver. I explained this to Joan as it could fail to start at any time.

Over the following two years many a male guest was amazed by Joan's mechanical wisdom. Often with a car full of guests, parked outside a venue in Washington, the car would refuse to start. Refusing assistance, Joan would calmly reach into the glove box and pull out an old screwdriver. Its metal stem was pitted from repeated jolts of electricity. After a male passenger turned the key on, she would open the hood and place the screwdriver over the two contact points. Within seconds the engine would roar to life. I was not there, but I would bet a knowing, broad smile creased her face as she closed the hood and returned to the car.

Knowing is not enough to be wise. Jesus said, "…who(ever) hears these words of mine and puts them into practice is like a wise man…" (Matthew 7:24) Many have read the Bible and heard Jesus' words, but unless they apply those words to their own life and practice, they remain foolish.

HERITAGE

"The boundary lines have fallen for me in pleasant places; surely I have a delightful inheritance."

PSALM 16:6

I was born the sixth son of Rev. Peter and Edith Holwerda. My given name came from my father's best friend, Dr. Harry Kok. My middle name, Lee, came from Lee Street Christian Reformed Church where my father was the pastor. At my retirement, many years later, my older brother David wrote, "Your name was prophetic, as medicine and church were the twin focuses of your life."

My father, a beloved pastor, exerted tremendous influence on his six sons. He never, however, attempted to force any of his sons to follow him in the ministry. He strongly, and rightly, believed that one can serve God in all walks of life. His was such a compelling example of Christian service, however, that four of the six sons chose to follow in his footsteps.

My oldest brother, George, served the church for forty years. The second oldest, Peter, was killed in France during World War II, before realizing his dream of ministry. Ironically, he was killed where my father stopped in World War I. The fourth son, Robert, also served the church for over forty years. The fifth son, David, served the church through his teaching at both the college and seminary level. His writing skills were extensively used by the church. The third and sixth sons, my brother Jack and I , kiddingly called ourselves the black sheep. Jack was anything but a black sheep. He served the church as an elder and was generous to a fault to those in need whether family or stranger. Eventually, three grandsons entered the ministry. Two, Peter and James, were sons of my brother George and the third is my son, Timothy.

"...Surely I have a delightful inheritance," (Psalm 6:16) because of a loving close family that modeled Christian service and taught it to their children. As Joshua said to the people of Israel, "Choose...whom you will serve,...but as for me and my household we will serve the Lord." Joshua. 24:15

Mt. SanGay volcano-Ecuador

THE PROMISE

"When you make a vow to God,
do not delay to fulfill it..."

ECCLESIASTES 5:4

As I grew up, the legacy of my father and older brothers was always before me. They modeled Christian service in the ministry. Teachers and fellow church members all assumed that I would follow suit. My vocation was a tacit assumption. I would enter the ministry like my father and brothers. Although I was interested in ministry, to some extent, I resented the assumption that others had made.

When I entered Calvin College in 1957, graduation from our denominational seminary required the mastery of three languages. The first was the Dutch of our heritage. A language in which many fine theological books had been written. The second and third languages were Hebrew and Greek, the languages of the Bible. I had studied Latin for two years in high school. Scholastically it had not been a problem, but I did not enjoy it. Three additional languages were not something I looked forward to.

I chose to study medicine and found chemistry and biology far more to my liking. My father was not upset, but encouraged me in my chosen profession. Deep in my own heart, however, I wondered if I was running from a deeper service to God. Little did I realize that medicine would provide countless opportunities for pastoring, witnessing, and Christian service, opportunities not as available to the pastors in my family. Almost all people experience sickness at one time or another and seek a physician's help. The relationships that develop from those experiences give the physician numerous opportunities to speak to the deeper and spiritual needs of his patients. When he speaks, it is as a trusted friend. As I pursued the medical profession, I promised God that I would go wherever He wanted me to go as a physician.

In wars, dangers, sickness and disasters, many are quick to promise God their love and service, if only they will be delivered. Be careful in what you promise and as the Psalmist says, "do not delay in fulfilling it." God will hold you to your promise.

DECISION

"If you make a vow to the LORD your God,
do not be slow to pay it, for the LORD your God
will certainly demand it of you..."

DEUTERONOMY 23:21

In 1968, I neared the end of my two years of active military duty. I had enjoyed my military service and would be eligible for a promotion if I continued. However, I really wanted more variety in patient care. Dr. John VanderMolen asked me to join him in his family practice in Grand Rapids, Michigan. He was a wonderful Christian as well as a physician highly respected at the hospital and by his patients. He told me to call when I had made up my mind and he would have the attorney draw up partnership papers.

While in Grand Rapids, I was also contacted by Dr. Henry Evenhouse, the director of Christian Reformed World Missions. He challenged me to take over the work of Dr. Ed Stehouwer, a long-term missionary in Nigeria. Nigeria was now engaged in a civil war and missionary doctors were in short supply. I met with the representatives of Christian Reformed World Missions, but did not sense a call to Africa. I had already been to the jungles of Ecuador and really preferred family practice in Grand Rapids to going to West Africa. Joan and I told the mission board we would prayerfully consider their request. We then returned to Andrews AFB. There we would complete our service and make a decision about reenlisting, going into family practice, or returning to the mission field.

The telephone in our apartment hung on the wall just inside the entrance to our kitchen. Nightly for the next three weeks, I walked into the kitchen with the intention of calling Dr. VanderMolen. Each night, for several minutes, I would stand there with the receiver in my hand unable to complete the call. I was uneasy about the decision to go into family practice rather than returning to the mission field. I began to feel that God was holding me to the promise I had made several years ago; a promise to go wherever He wanted me to go.

The uneasiness drove me to my knees. In the privacy of our bedroom, I prayed a simple but honest prayer, "Lord, I do not want to go to West Africa, but I will honor the promise I made to go wherever You want. If you want me in West Africa just give me peace with that decision." I had barely gotten off my knees when all doubts were gone. I walked back into the kitchen and said to Joan, "Hon, we are going to Africa." Private practice would have to wait.

"If you make a vow to the LORD your God...the LORD your God will certainly demand it of you..." (Deuteronomy 23:21) Do not promise what you are unwilling to fulfill!

FAITH OF OUR FATHERS

"If you believe, you will receive
whatever you ask for in prayer."

MATTHEW 21:22

Joan was supportive of the decision to go to West Africa. In her nurses' training she had also considered foreign mission service. My father, however, was surprised at my decision, as I had shown little interest in our previous conversations. This puzzled me.

Dad and Mom were then spending a few weeks in Florida with Dad's younger brother. He asked if Joan and I might come down for a few days for a thorough, relaxed discussion. As we had vacation days still coming, we arranged for a quick trip to Florida.

Dad wanted to know what had changed my mind. When he learned of the promise I had made in college and God's answer to my prayer, he was fully supportive. We had to go and be wherever God wanted us to be.

It was not until we returned from Africa three years later that we learned why my father was concerned about our decision. He had a dream soon after my decision to return to medical missions in Africa. In that dream I never returned, but died there. Dad shared the dream with my brother Bob and the two covenanted to not mention it to us. Having already lost a son in World War II, it was a stirring testimony to my father's faith. He believed I would die in Africa. But if that was where God wanted me, that was where I belonged.

I am sure both my father and my brother prayed more for our safety because of the knowledge of that dream. Joan and I returned in good health, but my father was to nearly die of stomach cancer before our return.

"I will go where you want me to go, Dear Lord," is the verse of a familiar hymn. Would you really go? Or do you first count the cost? Would you support your children or loved ones who felt God's call, even if you feared for their safety? Would you support them and place them in God's hand and pray diligently for them?

Rescue helicopter for President

RIOT

The 1968 riots and the multiple fires soon overwhelmed the Washington, D.C., police forces. Rioters ran freely in the streets while the firemen were unable to effectively fight the fires because of the violence. A request was made for the president to release military forces to help regain control of the city.

President Johnson immediately ordered the 82nd Airborne to be airlifted from North Carolina to Washington, D.C.. The air force base was put on alert. The flight surgeons were notified to prepare for twenty-four hour availability. They would be responsible for providing emergency care to the flight crews flying in and out of the base around the clock.

We all took turns standing by the flight line as this impressive operation took place. Huge cargo planes, C-130s or C-141s, landed every minute at the base. As one huge plane's wheels touched down, another plane turned into its final approach behind it. You could set your watch by it.

Immediately, after landing the aircraft taxied to the side and its massive doors opened. Inside, semi trucks full of combat ready troops were sitting side by side. As soon as the trucks cleared the aircraft, they headed for the gate and downtown Washington. The empty cargo plane closed its doors and immediately began a full power take off. Another aircraft immediately took its place at the side of the runway to discharge troops.

The airlift continued round-the-clock for forty-eight hours. The massive show of force soon controlled the rioting and the firemen gained control of the fires. I wondered what went through the minds of the soldiers as they reached the rioting black neighborhoods of the city because over 90 percent of the soldiers were also black.

"I have taken an oath and confirmed it..." (Psalm 119:106) The soldiers had taken an oath to uphold the laws of the United States. Although the rioters were their black brothers, they had pledged to obey the laws and would restore order. Christians pledge to love and honor the righteous laws of God. Do you uphold God's laws not only when others are doing so, but also when those laws are unpopular, mocked, or you are alone? "I have taken an oath and confirm it, that I will follow your righteous laws." Psalm 119:106

DEPTH PERCEPTION

"...They may be ever seeing but never perceiving,
and ever hearing but not understanding;
otherwise they might turn and be forgiven."

MARK 4:12

Washington, D.C., rarely gets a lot of snow, but several inches had fallen in the days before this incident. The runways had been plowed and several feet of snow was piled high on each side. Overnight, a light snowfall had again covered the runways with an inch or so of snow.

I saw the F-100 fighter plane as it approached for landing. The pilot flared the aircraft but it was far too high above the snow covered runway to land. The white runway with snow piled on each side had altered his depth perception. He saw the runway clearly, but did not perceive his height above it. As the aircraft slowed it got behind what is known as the power curve; the speed at which an aircraft can fly or stall. The pilot noting his error immediately added power in an attempt to fly around. The fighter plane was nearly standing on its tail and staggered like a drunk as more power was applied. Finally the plane leveled off, gained speed, and flew around.

In our training about aircraft accidents, we were shown a similar incident. That pilot was not as fortunate. As he got behind the power curve and the tail dropped, the aircraft somersaulted, nose first, over and over in a ball of flames. He was killed.

Later I saw the shaken pilot in the flight surgeon's office. Physically there were no problems to account for the near accident. His depth perception had been altered by the snow. He was still very anxious and his hands continued to shake. He was grateful to God because his life had been spared.

"...Seeing but never perceiving...hearing but not understanding..." (Mark 4:12) Jesus of course was not talking about landing aircraft. He was talking about the resistance and failure of people to see and understand His words and God's call. "...Ever hearing but not understanding, otherwise they might turn and be forgiven." (Mark 4:12)

Increasingly, here in the United States the perception of God's word is that it is no longer relevant. Like the pilot, unbelievers face death unless they turn and are forgiven.

MAN'S LEGS

"His pleasure is not in the strength of the horse,
nor his delight in the legs of the man;
the Lord delights in those who fear him,
who put their hope in his unfailing love."

PSALM147: 10-11

One of the delightful additions to military service in Washington, D.C., was our fellowship at the Washington, D.C., Christian Reformed Church. It always gave me a thrill when we exited the Beltway and saw the Capitol Building as we neared the church. The church was enriched by many couples now in military service and many others in long-term government service. It was a church with a warm fellowship which drew us all together as we grew spiritually

There were many young couples in the church, and we had an active sports program. In the summer we played fast pitch softball each week in a private league. I had played the game since early childhood and it was a favorite avocation. Game days were a family outing as the wives and children accompanied us to the ball field each week. There was always ice cream afterwards. That year we won the private league championship and were invited to a round-robin tournament in the State of Virginia. I still relish memories of those years of family time and softball in the company of wonderful acquaintances.

In the fall we played touch football in the same private league. The field was just beyond the trees separating us from the Lincoln Memorial. We were not as skilled as in softball but won more than we lost. I can still remember fading back to throw a pass and glimpsing the face of Abe Lincoln smiling down on us. The Vietnam War was only three years old and little did we realize that the casualties of that war would one day be permanently honored on the field on which we were playing.

"God does not delight in the legs of a man." God is not impressed with the abilities of man in sports or other activities. We, however, live in a culture that worships sports and man's abilities both mental and physical. More watch football than go to church each Sunday. Others worship at the throne of science. "…The LORD delights in them that fear him, and put their hope in his unfailing love." (Psalm 147:11) Man's abilities are limited and short lived. Fear God and put your trust in His unlimited abilities and everlasting love.

A LITTLE THING

"Who of you by worrying can add a single hour
to his life? Since you cannot do this very little thing,
why do you worry about the rest?"

LUKE 12:25-26

A t the end of June 1968, we completed our military service. We returned to Grand Rapids to begin our preparation for service in Nigeria. There were so many things to do and so little time before our departure in less than two months.

Nigeria was at war and this further limited what was available in the country. We poured over previous missionaries shipping lists and discussed with them what items needed to be sent on ahead. Supplies would be needed for the next three years including food, clothing, bedding, and numerous household items. As we began our purchasing, we were directed to several Christian businessmen who opened their businesses to missionaries. This stretched our limited outfitting budget and allowed us to buy in volume and often at wholesale prices. We expected to live primarily off of the food available in Nigeria. The food we brought with us would be a treat reminding us of home once or twice a month. But even a can or two a month was a lot of groceries over three years. Certain items, such as cake mixes, would be totally unavailable as were all other baking mixes. We would have to bring whatever we wanted.

Anticipating clothing needs was more difficult. Buying for Joan and I three years in advance was difficult enough. Anticipating the children's needs was far more difficult. How much would each grow in the next three years? What size clothing and what shoe sizes would they need? Should we plan for another addition? What one gift should we include for their birthdays and for three Christmases?

Did we worry? I am sure we did, usually whether we had enough or the right sizes. The text is a wonderful reminder about our useless worrying. All of us do it, before and often after events. "Who of you, by worrying, can add one hour to your life? Since you cannot do this very little thing why do you worry about the rest?" (Luke 12:25-26) Memorize this text and use it whenever worrying over comes you.

BARRELS

"Do not store up for yourselves treasures on earth,
where moths and rust destroy,
and where thieves break in and steal."

MATTHEW 6:19

Rapidly our supplies accumulated in the basement of Joan's family home. I now needed to find enough barrels in which to ship them. I was given the name of a dock foreman at the large Nabisco cookie factory in Grand Rapids. For a reasonable price I purchased thirteen, fifty-five gallon barrels. All were in good condition and several were new. Most had a plastic liner to contain the honey and jam shipped to the factory. All had a metal cover with a lock.

One by one I rolled the barrels into the backyard and began scrubbing the sticky residue from their insides. It took a lot of elbow grease and even more hot water. The barrels would not only be useful in shipping, but also for storage in Africa. We literally had to protect our "treasures" from moths and rust as well as insects, rats, snakes, and thieves.

Joan and I had packed numerous suitcases before, but this was our first attempt at packing barrels. Everything from cases of vegetables, clothing, household items and even chocolate chips was packed inside. It would be a long sea voyage before our barrels reached Africa. It would begin in Chicago, then up the St. Lawrence Seaway, and across the Atlantic Ocean to Lagos, Nigeria. The barrels would take months to reach Africa, so we brought them to the shipper several weeks before we were to leave.

We were not storing up earthly treasures, but basic necessities for living during our work in Africa. The text of course was Jesus' warning about a life of accumulating possessions here on earth; possessions that could be stolen from us or destroyed by various processes of aging. Possessions we could not keep in this life or carry to the next. Rather, Jesus added, "store up treasures in heaven." The gospels stress generously sharing what we have with others, particularly the poor. Do you generously share what you have with others in need?

MORE THAN

"Anyone who loves their father or mother more
than me is not worthy of me; anyone who loves his
son or daughter more than me is not worthy of me;
and anyone who does not take up their cross
and follow me is not worthy of me.
Whoever finds his life will lose it, and whoever
loses their life for my sake will find it."

MATTHEW 10:37-39

One of the most difficult aspects of foreign missionary service is leaving behind family and friends. Separation is always difficult, but when it is to be for years it is all the more so. For two weeks all of my brothers and their families along with Mom and Dad camped with us on the shores of Lake Michigan. Camping was one of our family traditions, and we would miss seeing them and camping with them for the next three years. Joan's parents with her brother and her sister's family also came to visit with us. The vacation passed far too quickly and soon we were all saying goodbye.

A few days later Joan and I packed our bags in anticipation of a night flight to Europe. However, our Nigerian visa's had not yet arrived. Then at noon we were notified that the visa's had come and we proceeded to the airport.

With tears in our eyes and the voices of friends and family ringing in our ears, we walked out onto the tarmac and boarded the plane. As the plane taxied down the runway, we glanced back at the terminal building where family and friends continued to wave. We had left them before for three months. This time it would be three years.

"Anyone who loves their father or mother more than me is not worthy of me..." (Matthew 10:37) Jesus is not telling us to not love our parents or children or brothers or sisters. Our first love, however, is to Him; a love shown by the willingness to give up all that we have and all that is dear to us so we may serve Him. A willingness to pick up our cross and do what is required of us. We do not find our lives by seeking all we can in this temporal world. We find our life by losing it for His sake!

Joan, Christy and Tim

Outpatient clinic, Takum Christian Hospital

Harry, Christy and Tim by their home

ALL

*"And my God will meet all your needs according
to the riches of his glory in Christ Jesus."*

PHILIPPIANS 4:19

When we left for Africa, many missionary friends suggested that we take some time to visit some of the countries we were passing through. As Joan and I had never before traveled in Europe, this seemed like a wonderful opportunity. We spent a few days in Amsterdam, then several beside Lake Lucerne in Switzerland before traveling to Germany. Christy and Tim, our two small children, traveled amazingly well. We only wished at times they were a bit older so they too could enjoy all that we were seeing.

In Germany, we had been invited to spend three days with an old friend and his family from the air force. Andy Nemanis and I served together in the flight surgeons office at Andrews AFB for nearly two years. He had been transferred to Stuttgart, Germany, a month before we finished our service. He knew of our plans and insisted that we stop and visit with them on our way to Africa.

Andy and I spent many hours together at Andrews AFB, and we had also socialized with him and his wife, Judy. They were not Christians, although Andy and I had some deep spiritual chats. He had remarked once, "I wish I could believe like that." Joan and I were concerned about living in their home for three days. Would we all feel uncomfortable spending that much time together? Joan and I prayed that God would allow the families to be comfortable together, that we could be a Christian witness and not offend their generous hospitality.

A week before our arrival, one of the colonels at the base was sent for a mental evaluation to Andy's office. Stuttgart, Germany, was then the command center for the USAF. The colonel held a highly sensitive position. For the past few months he had been speaking in tongues and sharing his faith with many, including generals. Andy had to decide if he was a security risk and/or mentally ill.

Andy met us at the airport literally with an open Bible in his hands. "And my God will meet all your needs according to the riches of his glory in Christ Jesus." (Philippians 4:19) We had worried about what we would talk about for three days and whether we would make them uncomfortable if we shared our faith. God had them waiting with an open Bible and many questions. Is your God too small? Is there anything too small or too big to bring to Him in prayer? "...My God will meet all your needs according to the riches of his glory in Christ Jesus." Philippians 4:19

TONGUES

*"Other languages, then, are meant to be a sign,
not for believers but for unbelievers."*

1 CORINTHIANS 14:22

The colonel in Dr. Nemanis's office was a new Christian who had asked God to affirm the truth of scripture by having him speak in tongues. To his great surprise, his request was answered. My friend, Andy, had a good ear for language. His family had been Lithuanian immigrants who fled to the United States when the Iron Curtain dropped on Eastern Europe. Andy spoke Lithuanian, French, and English and he was impressed by the colonel's testimony and by the recordings of him speaking in tongues. Andy was convinced that the colonel was speaking a language and not gibberish.

We had wondered how we would witness to our friends as we lived in their home for three days. We should not have been surprised that God had them waiting with a Bible. Speaking in tongues is neither a spiritual gift I possess nor a gift I have sought, but it opened the door for witnessing to Andy and his wife. They asked repeated questions about the Christian faith. The conversations were comfortable and only deepened our relationship rather than being a source of tension. I was asked to daily lead family devotions at the table. I shared I Corinthians 14:22 with Andy and told him that I personally did not feel speaking in tongues was necessary to be a Christian.

Andy and his wife were most gracious as our host and hostess. They arranged babysitting at the base so we could sight see together while the children played. Our children enjoyed playing far more than sightseeing. They drove us to various places in Germany and treated us at various restaurants. One day we drove over the border to visit my brother's grave in France. Our hosts insisted on paying all of the expenses. Whenever I took out my wallet, Andy would stop me and say, "You cannot pay. You are missionaries. Let me pay for you."

The Apostle Paul said, "Tongues, then, are a sign not for believers but for unbelievers..." (I Corinthians 14:22) Andy had seen that sign in a fellow officer. Andy and his wife continued to express a wish to believe. Pray for them.

Examing patient in TB compound

I HAVE KEPT THE FAITH

"I have fought the good fight, I have finished
the race, I have kept the faith. ⁸ Now there is in store
for me the crown of righteousness, which the Lord,
the righteous Judge, will award to me on that day
—and not only to me, but also to all who
have longed for his appearing."

2 TIMOTHY 4:7-8

We crossed the bridge at Saarbrucken, Germany, and entered into France. Our hosts had brought wine, bread, and cheese to share along the roadside. After lunch we proceeded to the U.S. Military cemetery at St. Avod, France. My brother, Peter, was buried there after he had been killed at Metz in 1944. Metz was also where our father, Peter, stopped at the end of World War I.

An American officer met us at the reception center. He looked for the location of Peter's grave in a large book. He soon found it and drove us there in a golf cart. Over 22,000 American servicemen are buried there. It is a sad, but impressive, sight viewing row upon row of white marble crosses that form straight lines from all angles.

The officer then took some sand from a bucket and rubbed it into Peter's name chiseled on the marble cross. The sand made his name stand out against the white marble and, therefore, easily visible in our many pictures. Amazingly, the remains of soldiers from that war twenty-three years ago are still being recovered from the farms and hedgerows of Europe.

I was nearly five years old when I answered the doorbell early one morning in 1944. A messenger from Western Union stood on the doorstep and asked for my father. I raced upstairs to get him and stood with him in the doorway as he read the telegram. My father wept openly, and I cried with him. I had never seen my father weep before.

I have a few fond memories of Peter mostly from his furloughs before being shipped overseas. I remember being the first one to see him walking around the church on his last furlough. I raced to meet him and was embraced in his arms. Most of my memories, however, come from old photographs, letters, and the memories of others.

I wish I could have spent more time with my brother. By all accounts he was a wonderful Christian, mature far beyond his years. His Captain wrote my father after my brother's death and said, "He was a nigh perfect youth." His last act was caring for a wounded German soldier and waving for a jeep before the sniper shot and killed him. Later in life I met two of Peter's friends who entered the ministry to take his place. "I have fought the good fight, I have finished the race, I have kept the faith." (II Timothy 4:7) May I run and finish as well!

AFRICA

*"'Leave your country and your people,'" God said,
'and go to the land I will show you.'"*

ACTS 7:3

The 707 airliner flew south out of Rome, Italy. For hours we flew through the night above the vast Sahara Desert. The desert separated the ancient cities and development of Northern Africa from the African Sudan below the desert. In the darkness little was visible from the plane. Occasionally, the lights of a small settlement or city temporarily lit the landscape below. But for most of the night, the vast desert was unmarked by the lights of civilization.

British Airways made the only flights into Nigeria and these flights were only twice a week. Each arrived late at night and as soon as the planes were refueled they left again with any departing passengers. Around midnight we arrived in Kano, Nigeria, an ancient walled city on the southern edge of the Sahara Desert. The city was over 800 years old and was still a regular destination of camel caravans crossing the desert.

The next morning we left for the even smaller city of Jos and the headquarters of Christian Reformed World Missions.

The morning flight was aboard an old Ford Tri-motor. The plane looked as if it had flown out of a newsreel taken in the 1930's. The passenger compartment was narrow with small uncomfortable seats and little leg room. The aircraft rattled continuously and the noise of its three motors prevented normal conversation. In the tropical heat, there was no air conditioning. Fresh air blew through the plane from two small windows at the front of the aircraft; small windows, like those in the front doors of old cars that could be angled out to direct air into the car.

Jos was not our final destination, but the city where we would begin our acclimation to the country and people we had been called to serve. In a week we would fly hundreds of miles into the "bush" to our home in Africa.

"Leave your country and people..." (Acts 7:3) God called Abraham out of Ur of the Chaldeas and has been calling His people to serve Him ever since. Many are called to serve right at home among their own people. Do you serve? Others are called to distant lands and people. It is hard to leave. Would you go? Would you let your children go? That is also hard. But when God calls, "Leave your country and your people... and go to the land I will show you." (Acts 7:3) Those called must go and those left behind must support them, even if it is hard.

FAMILY

" I tell you the truth," Jesus replied, "no one
who has left home or brothers or sisters or mother
or father or children or fields for me
and the gospel will fail to receive a hundred times
as much in this present age..."

MARK 10:29-30

We were excited as we boarded the small Piper Aztec for the last leg of our journey. Tim nestled in his mother's lap while Christy sat next to them. I sat next to the pilot, Ray Browneye, in the remaining front seat of the plane. The plane also carried new supplies bought in Jos. Some of them were ours, the rest intended for other missionaries in the bush.

The small village of Takum is located about 350 miles southeast of Jos and sixty miles from the border of the French Cameroons. The area around Takum is known as the "bush", not only for its isolation, but also because of the stunted small trees that grow there. The trees rarely attain full growth because each year they are burned. Lacking farming equipment, the farmers annually burned the tall grasses off of their fields to prepare for planting. For weeks the entire countryside was ablaze.

Although the sun was shining, its light was dimmed by the particles of sand that filled the air. Ray said it was the beginning of the Harmattan season; a season when strong winds blew across the desert and filled the air with sand. It reached great heights and when thick, the sand so markedly decreased visibility that planes could not fly.

Two hours later we glimpsed the small village of Takum. A single unpaved road ran through its center, while small mud huts surrounded it. A half -mile away a cluster of long, white, rectangular buildings indicated the location of Takum Christian Hospital.

Ray set the plane down on the short dirt runway. We had arrived at our new home and others soon overwhelmed us with a warm welcome. Christy and Tim stood closely by our sides firmly clasping our hands. Who were all these new people? Little did the children realize how soon they would be their loved surrogate uncles, aunts, and grandparents. God was faithfully providing brothers, sisters, mothers, fathers, and a new family. The missionaries would be part of our new family while an even larger portion would come from those we came to serve.

"I tell you the truth," Jesus replied, "no one who has left home or brothers or sisters or mother or father or children or fields for me and the gospel will fail to receive a hundred times as much in this present age..." Mark 10:29-30

FEAR

"You will tread upon the lion and the cobra;
you will trample the great lion and the serpent."

PSALM 91:13

There is only one poisonous snake in the State of Michigan. It is a pygmy rattlesnake who is infrequently encountered and whose venom rarely causes death. In the area surrounding our home in Takum, Nigeria, there were five species of poisonous snakes, all of whose venom was deadly.

After our welcome at the airport, we stopped at the home of Dr. Herm Grey. He was now the only physician in Takum following Dr. Stehouwer's departure. He quickly invited us into his backyard to show us what had been discovered on the mission compound that day.

Dr. Grey, in addition to being a physician, was an amateur ornithologist and herpetologist. In other words, he loved to watch birds and he loved snakes. As we walked around the house I saw the two large, bright green snakes laying dead on the grass. Each was over five feet in length. Herm informed us that they had been killed in the backyard of our new home that morning. Since the Stehouwer's departure six weeks ago, no one had lived in our home and the grass was uncut until today.

"These are not, however, the deadly Green Mambas," Herm explained. "They are just identical in appearance to the untrained eye." Lifting one snake to eye level and holding out its head, Herm explained, "See, you can tell the difference by counting the scales underneath the eye."

If this was meant to reassure us, it certainly did not have that effect on my wife, Joan. She stood silently, tightly gripping a hand of each of our small children who were two and four years old. The tears would come later that day along with an overwhelming fear that she could never let the children out of the house again.

"You will tread upon the lion and the cobra..." (Psalm 91:13) Psalm 91 is a wonderful testimony to the security and protection God gives to those who trust in Him. Trust in God. Who else could protect us here? Alone we were helpless. Missionaries from our church have been here in Africa since the 1930s. When we arrived in 1968, the group had grown to 168 adult missionaries, with their families, in 18 mission stations. No one, in all those years, had ever been bitten by a snake! Trust in God!

DAILY BREAD

"Give us each day our daily bread."

LUKE 11:3

Until our arrival in the bush, neither Joan nor I worried much about our daily bread. Stores were convenient and bread readily available nearly everywhere. Joan baked bread only on special occasions or holidays.

There were no bakeries or places to buy bread in the bush. Joan would have to bake bread three times a week. It would be a challenge as her stove had only an old iron oven that burned wood. An oven probably identical to the one her grandmother used.

The fresh bread was certainly not part of my sacrifice for living in the bush. However, from Joan's perspective it was a difficult chore. The flour came in 100-pound sacks that were invariably full of weevils. Each cup of flour had to be sifted before baking, always leaving a telltale pile of weevils on the countertop. I joked about the protein the weevils could add to the bread, but Joan was not amused. The yeast was not always active and the shortening only a margarine "like" substance. It was called "Blue Bonnet" and came in fifty pound tins. It was known as "axle grease" in the mission community. It was palatable in small amounts, especially if cold. However, it rapidly separated into its various ingredients if heated.

Joan soon mastered the wood stove, although she said it continued to frustrate her. Her fresh bread was delicious, and I can almost still taste the hot wheat, cinnamon, and raisin breads that came from her oven. Eventually, she trained one of our house boys to bake bread. His strong hands could more easily knead the dough. Joan taught him well and his bread was nearly as good as hers.

"Give us each day our daily bread." (Luke 11:3) In the text from the gospel of Luke, "bread" does not refer only to the bread eaten each day. It is much broader and refers to everything needed to sustain our lives. In the Lord's Prayer, Jesus is encouraging us to acknowledge our daily dependence on the Father. We do not ask for tomorrow, but must daily ask Him to sustain us day by day.

Children always drew a crowd

CLEAN AND UNCLEAN

"Are you still so dull?" Jesus asked them. "Don't you
see that whatever enters the mouth goes into the
stomach and then out of the body? But the things
that come out of the mouth come from the heart,
and these make a man unclean. For out of the heart
come evil thoughts—murder, adultery, sexual
immorality, theft, false testimony, slander."

MATTHEW 15:16-19

Once each week, meat was butchered near the market in the village of Takum. The Muslim butchers had religious restrictions on what they might eat, similar to the old Jewish laws on clean and unclean. Those laws were addressed by Jesus in the text today. Those restrictions, however, did not prevent them from butchering and selling the meat to others.

There was little variety at the market. Beef was most commonly available and occasionally pork, goat, or fish. Without refrigeration, whatever was butchered was sold and eaten that day. The butchering was crude. The carcass of the animal was simply laid down in the dust and dirt. There were no cuts of meat. The meat was simply stripped from the carcass or torn off the bones in chunks.

There was one modern convenience—home delivery. After an animal was butchered, a young man would make rounds of all the mission homes on the compound. He carried the meat in a metal bucket on top of his head and carried a scale in his other hand. As Joan wrote in a letter home, "The meat man came by this morning with a scale and a big pail of meat. The meat had been sitting in the hot sun since early morning. He weighed out a large piece—there were no cuts only globs of meat. It sells for twenty-eight cents a pound without bones. It is very sandy and dirty and must be washed thoroughly before putting it away. Once it is clean, it doesn't look too bad but rarely tastes very good. It has a peculiar taste no matter how you doctor it up. It is very tough and must be pressure cooked to be eaten."

We had no dietary laws or religious restrictions on what we ate. There were no spiritual consequences to eating all sorts of meats although the meat itself was physically very unclean. Jesus was changing the age old laws of the Jewish people in regards to what is clean or unclean. What enters a man 's mouth does not make a him unclean but the evil that comes out of his mouth, that makes him unclean. Later in the chapter Jesus explains that what comes out of our mouths comes from our sinful hearts. It is not what we touch, but our sinful hearts that make all of us unclean.

WHY?

"...Who can say to Him, 'What are you doing?'"

JOB 9:12

It was a great relief when our new refrigerator arrived in Takum on one of the mission's lorries. We were very excited, and after borrowing a crowbar, I attacked the crate. The refrigerator was not as large as we had hoped but would do nicely. It even had a small freezer compartment atop the shelves.

Unlike the electric refrigerators back home, this refrigerator was powered by kerosene. A metal container under the refrigerator held a bit more than one gallon of fuel. This was enough for about two weeks. Each time the container was refilled, a wick atop the container needed to be trimmed and relit.

The refrigerator was a great source of interest to our African friends. One day Joan burned her fingers on the oven and prepared a bowl of ice water to sooth them. Christy and Tim were always eager to play with ice cubes and gave them to their African playmates. None of them had ever seen an ice cube before. Their first response was to drop it. It was colder than anything they had ever touched. Then they began to giggle as they played with it. Then it disappeared. Why?

One night one of my African surgical assistants dropped by the house to greet me. I was in the process of relighting the refrigerator and had just given him a glass of cold water. He watched me light the refrigerator and then asked a very perceptive question. "Likita" (Doctor), why when I light a fire does everything get hot and when you light a fire everything gets cold?" I tried to explain the physics of the expansion and contraction of freon gas. I am sure he did not fully understand as that subject had certainly not been covered in an education that went only through the third grade.

Job's life is now in shambles and he has lost everything. Job chapter 9 is a beautiful testimony to the greatness of God. But Job wants to know why, he does not understand.

"...Who can say to Him, 'What are you doing?'" (Job 9:12) How many times in your life have you asked God, why? It is a common question. Later God gave Job an education and Job had no more questions. Like my African friends, like Job, we often want to know why things happen to us. We ask God, "What are you doing? I don't understand, why?" Because we are finite human beings, we often can't understand. We often must be content with the knowledge that we belong to a faithful Savior and that all He does works out for our salvation.

WASTE

*"When the disciples saw this, they were indignant.
'Why this waste?' they asked."*

MATTHEW 26:8

Occasionally, the missionaries would butcher an entire cow for themselves. After the cow was killed, its carcass was hung from the peak of the carpenters shed. The animal was skinned and the head and intestines piled atop the hide, which now lay on the ground. The carcass was then split, with a skill saw, before butchering. The Africans would often laugh about all the parts we threw away. They felt it terribly wasteful. They were extremely grateful when the "waste" was given to them.

I had a similar experience when I visited a medical clinic in the town of Ibi. It is a fishing village and lies next to the Benue River. After a day helping the medical worker at the clinic, I wandered down to the market. I hoped to buy fish for those on our compound. Fresh fish was a real a treat to those of us in the bush nearly 100 miles away.

It was a very good day of fishing on the river, and I quickly purchased nearly forty pounds of fish. I wanted them cleaned before taking them with us on the mission plane that evening. Two of the men volunteered to help me. Africans don't clean the fish before eating as we do. I had an African meal at lunch. The wife of the young clinic worker had served us a stew with the meat a mixture of goat's lung and fish. The goat's lung was a gift from the Muslim village chief. I had asked his permission to work there that morning. The fish was bought in the market and then cut into cross sections before being added to the stew. It tasted fine, once I overcame my surprise at seeing that the cross sections of fish also included their bowels.

As we squatted on the ground, a growing pile of fish heads and innards grew large between us. As we worked, my two African helpers continued to laugh and shake their heads. What a waste! The local evangelist was delighted with my gift of "waste."

The disciples felt it a waste when the woman poured a whole bottle of perfume on Jesus' feet. I was struck by how the Africans made use of everything. I come from a society sometimes known as a throw-away society. We throw away enormous amounts of just about everything, including food. Our garbage dumps are filled to overflowing so we dig new ones. What a waste! I am not asking that you begin to eat chitlins and chew animal hide, but I would like you to look at your lifestyle and cut down on all that you waste.

TRAINING

"May the favor of the Lord our God rest on us;
establish the work of our hands for us—yes,
establish the works of our hands."

PSALM 90:17

The volume of work at the Takum Christian Hospital was staggering. The beds for 180 inpatients were constantly full and many lay on the floor. During the week, there were more than 400 outpatients daily. On Saturday and Sunday only emergency patients were seen. There was an average of fifteen major surgeries each week along with even more minor procedures. In addition, thirty patients with active Tuberculosis were treated, and cared for, in a separate compound.

My surgical experiences had been limited to my internship. I had expressed an interest in medical missions so the surgeons had given me a broad exposure to hernias, appendectomies, and bowel resections. I had only assisted. In three months, I was to have nearly complete responsibility for all the surgeries at the hospital.

Fortunately, Dr. Harvey Bratt, a board certified general surgeon, was able to spend the next three months with me.

He was on one of his many short-term mission trips. He was an excellent and patient instructor. He maintained a steady calm even in the face of difficult surgical problems and poor limited resources. The plan for my "surgical residency" was simple. We would operate daily, and I would assist on all emergencies, day and night. Over the following three months we performed over 230 major operations along with many minor procedures. Initially, I was the surgical assistant. After the first thirty cases, I became the surgeon while Dr. Bratt acted as my first assistant.

When I retired from medicine thirty-seven years later, Dr. Bratt wrote me reflecting on our time together. "1968 brought our lives together for a time in Nigeria. One of my assignments was to introduce a new young colleague to the challenges of surgery in the tropics. I must say that type of an assignment was a difficult one for me. I had to first adapt myself to the realities and limitations of third world surgery. Then teach all I had learned in a five year surgical residency to you in just a few months. It is a good thing you were an eager and apt pupil. You were always ready to take hold of a challenge sometimes a bit before you were properly equipped to do so. I remember having to hold you back a bit and having to tell you to observe this one more time before tackling it on your own. I appreciated your drive to learn and to take hold of things."

"May the favor of the Lord our God rest on us; establish the work of our hands for us..." (Psalm 90:17) The psalmist prayed that God would make the work of his hands effective and lasting. That should be the daily prayer of each us. Some work at home and others in various occupations. Unless God blesses and establishes what we do, we labor in vain. Do you pray for His favor and blessing on the work of your hands?

ADJUSTMENT

*"See the LORD your God has given you the land.
Go up and take possession of it as the Lord,
the God of your fathers told you Do not be afraid;
do not be discouraged."*

DEUTERONOMY 1:21

Adjustment to life in Africa was quite easy for me. I was immediately immersed in learning general surgery. Daily I saw complex surgical cases along with the most fascinating tropical diseases one could imagine. It was an incredible, life changing experience.

The adjustment for Joan was more difficult. She still had to run the home and mind the children with limited resources. Most of what we had was borrowed from neighbors, and daily there were still things we needed and had to borrow once again. All of the cooking was from scratch and very time intensive. Many of the foodstuffs and ingredients she had never seen before. The native ground rice contained bits of gravel from the grinding stone while the flour was full of weevils. Cooking on a wood-burning stove was also frustrating, and her household help spoke no English.

The children required extra time and patience as they too adjusted to new people and a sometimes puzzling environment. Their adjustment to the natives was aggravated by the African's curiosity about their white skin, blue eyes, and blond hair. The Africans could not resist the temptation to touch their skin and hair. The children found this irritating and often frightening.

Joan's anxiety over the snakes made her especially watchful of the children. She had not forgotten the two large snakes killed in our yard the day of our arrival. During the following six weeks, a cobra, a carpet viper, and a non-poisonous tree snake had also been killed elsewhere on the compound. It was difficult not to be afraid or discouraged.

Needless to say, tears of frustration were common during the first few months. Family support was limited to a husband who seemed to spend every waking minute at the hospital. But yet God was faithful. He provided a wonderful neighbor, Mrs. Helen Scholten. She and her husband had already spent many years in Nigeria. She understood Joan's tears and aggravation from her own experiences. She was a loving, patient, surrogate mother.

"...Do not be afraid; do not be discouraged." (Deuteronomy 1:21) Fear and discouragement are universal human feelings. None of us escapes them. All of us at sometime struggle with those feelings even though we know God is in control. How dependent we are. Pray daily for His Grace and encouragement.

LAWLESSNESS

"We also know that the law is made not for
the righteous but for lawbreakers and rebels,
the ungodly and sinful, the unholy and irreligious,
for those who kill their fathers or mothers,
for murderers, for adulterers and perverts,
for slave traders and liars and perjurers..."

1 TIMOTHY 1:9-10

M any tribes considered the area around Takum to be their home. When the British took over Nigeria in the mid-nineteenth century, most of these tribes lived atop hills or mountains. This was done for protection against other tribes engaged in slave trading. Although the British outlawed slave trading in their colonies in 1807, it persisted here well into the twentieth century. Slave trading continued because of raids by northern Muslims against the tribes of southern Nigeria.

One day I made a visit to the village of Bete thirty miles from Takum. It was isolated and accessible only by plane or foot. One of our pharmacy technicians accompanied me to the village. While in the village he pointed out a high mountain peak above us. "I was born at the base of that peak," he said.

British rule of law brought British justice and the British ordered all of the tribes down from their isolated mountain homes. The transition took time. Rev. Edgar Smith, a pioneer missionary in the work in the Sudan, tells this story about his trek to the village of Furam in 1930. "The path was narrow and dangerous. After hours of sweating upward in the tropical heat the path petered out. At that point we approached the protective device the villagers had devised. A tree trunk and another beyond it were suspended by ropes from above. Each man, facing a sheer rock wall, had to step first unto one tree trunk and then the other one edging slowly across to the other side. A false step would precipitate a fall of a thousand feet to death below. Each night and at times of danger, the drawbridge was removed."

Slowly, British law and protection extended across the country and proved dependable. Eventually, all of the tribes moved from the mountain tops to the valleys and plains below.

"We also know that the law is made not for the righteous but for lawbreakers and rebels..." (I Timothy 9) Lawlessness is still common in Africa. Think about the people of Somalia, the Congo, and Sudan. Murder, rape, and pillage are almost daily occurrences against defenseless individuals. Are you grateful for the police forces and courts of law that defend you daily? Do you pray and thank God for them? Do you daily pray for those who live without that protection?

WATER

*"...They camped at Rephidim, but there was no water
for the people to drink. So they quarreled with Moses
and said, 'Give us water to drink'..."*

EXODUS 17:1-2

Missionaries, who lived here for several years, told us the rainfall this year had not been as heavy as usual. The wells where we obtained water for the hospital and our personal use were not filled. The dry season would soon be upon us. Whether there was enough water or not, it would not rain again for four months. We were dependent upon the rains for water.

The water we received was pumped from two wells into a tank standing on a small rise near the hospital. It then flowed by gravity into our homes with very little pressure. The water was often red with dirt. It was not safe for drinking as it was contaminated by various bacteria and protozoa. Providing a drink of water was far more complicated than turning on the tap.

It took Joan about two hours to provide safe drinking water. First the water was boiled for ten minutes on the wood-burning stove. Then it was filtered through a stone filter of British design. It took thirty or more minutes for the water to filter through. One now had clean water, but it was still hot; fine for coffee, but not for young children. The water was now placed in the kerosene refrigerator for cooling. Each time more water was needed, the above process had to be repeated. Thirsty or not, at times we had to wait for a drink of clean water.

Coming from North American, neither Joan nor I ever thought much about a drink of water. It was available almost everywhere, from the tap in our home to drinking fountains on the street. One could safely drink the water from nearly every well, tap, or fountain in the country. Many people commonly drink out of their garden hose on a hot day.

Yet in the twenty-first century one of the greatest growing needs of the peoples of the world is water fit to drink. "...Give us water to drink..." (Exodus 17:2) In Africa and in almost all developing countries including India and China, there is little safe water for the people to drink. Most of it is untreated and contaminated with bacteria and protozoa, organisms that can cause severe diarrhea and death. Please support efforts by missions and other organizations as they attempt to provide water for people to drink. The cry is getting louder, "Give us water to drink."

CANNIBALS

*"You have heard that it was said to the people
long ago,' Do not murder, and anyone who
murders will be subject to judgment.'
But I tell you that anyone who is angry with his
brother will be subject to judgment..."*

MATTHEW 5:21-22

One of the largest tribes living in and around Takum Christian Hospital was the Kuteb people. The area has long been one of their ancestral homes. When Johanna Veenstra pioneered work in this area in 1921, she set up her first mission station at Lupwe about four miles from Takum.

There were no roads in the area, only bush paths surrounded by tall grasses and foliage. Johanna and the other women who joined her were warned about the dangers of the Kuteb. In those early days the Kuteb people were known as the "Dzompere," a word meaning "to eat a man." They were cannibals.

When my family and I came to Africa in 1968, my nearest African neighbor was a Kuteb man known as Jotto. He lived across the narrow dirt road that wound around the mission compound. His compound consisted of several mud huts with thatched roofs around a central clearing. By now he was a very elderly man. Through an interpreter, he shared his memories of his youth when his people were cannibals many years earlier.

A year later Jotto died. He was not a Christian. For many months there were weekly all- night celebrations as the Kuteb people danced around his grave. Occasionally, a special dance group came and we were invited to watch the ceremony. Amazingly, we learned to sleep, although the drums continued throughout the night.

"You have heard that it was said to the people long ago, '"Do not murder, and anyone who murders will be subject to judgment.' But I tell you that anyone who is angry with his brother will be subject to judgment..." (Matthew 5:21-22) We are shocked by the knowledge that people murdered and once ate others. Yet Jesus puts our anger in the same category as murder. None of us would think of practicing cannibalism. How many of us are never angry with a brother or sister? Do we destroy another's life with our anger?

Harry and Dr. Harvey Bratt

EMPATHY

"Rejoice with those who rejoice;
mourn with those who mourn."

ROMANS 12:15

O n a daily basis we saw new patients with tetanus. The majority were newborn infants. Death was very common, and we averaged one or more deaths from tetanus each and every day. Those infants whose symptoms occurred when they were a week or more of age had the best chance of survival. We saved over 40 percent of them. We never saw infants survive if the symptoms of tetanus occurred before they were a week of age.

Death after childbirth is heartbreaking. This is especially true in a culture where wives are valued by the number of living children they produce. Many children meant more hands to work the fields and to perform the hard manual labor associated with farming. In Nigeria it was the women and children who did the majority of this hard work.

African mothers, like mothers everywhere, love their children. The daily deaths of children were immediately accompanied by the wailing of their mothers and their relatives. The shrill screams pierced the silence of the hospital as the pain of death wrapped itself around a mother's heart. I will never forget those cries of pain for they pierced my heart as well.

Soon after an infant's death a small pathetic procession made its way from the hospital. A few friends and relatives hurried along the path with the mother. Her back was bent as she clutched a small bundle. Her dead infant wrapped tightly in a towel or blanket wet with her tears.

Burial comes quickly in the tropics for they had no means of preserving the body. A hole is quickly prepared and the bundle quickly placed in the ground. As the mother turns to leave the gravesite, she squeezes a few drops of milk from her breasts upon the grave; a last gift for the dead child.

"Rejoice with those who rejoice; mourn with those who mourn." (Romans 12:15) Rejoicing is easy. Mourning is difficult. Yet it is the Christian's privilege to identify with others in their joys and in their sorrows. Many avoid those who mourn because they don't know what to say. Most often it is not what we say but that we cared enough to be with them. It is enough to share their tears and to comfort them with our presence.

UNDERSTANDING

*"Give me understanding, and I will keep your law
and obey it with all my heart."*

PSALM 119:34

The numerous daily deaths from tetanus were difficult to accept. We all felt there must be a way to lower the mortality rate. At one point we thought we had the perfect solution. In health classes, rural nurses were already instructing the women about the causes of tetanus and the necessity of cleanliness at birth. In addition, we began supplying the outlying villages with small sterile packets. In each packet was a sterile shoestring and a sterile razor blade. The women in each village and the midwives were instructed to tie the cord with the sterile shoestring and then cut the cord with the sterile razor blade. They were forbidden to use their old hair scissors or other dirty sharp instruments.

The incidences of tetanus continue unabated. An ancient treatment was responsible. The African tribes, like people everywhere, were in the habit of applying poultices to wounds, sores, and umbilical cords. It was a custom that would take years to eliminate.

Poultices go back to the earliest civilizations. They are usually soft and composed of various herbs felt to have healing abilities. They may be applied hot or cold. They were often placed over open wounds or festering sores. To a twenty-first century reader, this may seem to be very primitive medicine. Yet today, millions of Americans are avid users of poultices. The most common poultice is "Bag Balm." It is an ointment used by farmers to treat the teats of their cows. Among patients it is known as "drawing salve."

The concept of sterility, in the face of open wounds or festering sores, is a difficult one to understand. Millions of Americans still don't get it. While "Bag Balm" is clean, it is not sterile, and the balm is contaminated each time a non-sterile finger draws it from the container. Our African friends had a much more severe problem. The main ingredient of their poultices was cow manure.

"Give me understanding, and I will keep your law and obey it..." (Psalm 119:34) Our African friends could follow our instructions, but they did not understand. In Matthew's gospel, Jesus speaks about those who hear, but do not understand. Do you "understand" what the Bible teaches you about how you should live? It is not enough to hear the words if you do not have understanding. Pray that you may hear and UNDERSTAND.

THE DARK CONTINENT

"The people living in darkness have seen
a great light; on those living in the land of the
shadow of death a light has dawned."

MATTHEW 4:16

I n the nineteenth century, Africa was known as the Dark Continent. This did not reflect the color of its people or that its environment lacked sunshine; it was known as the Dark Continent because the European world had little knowledge of it. Although much was known of the ancient cities and civilizations north of the Sahara Desert, little of the country south and east of the great desert had been explored.

One important reason prevented the European's exploration of these portions of Africa. West Africa was known as the white man's grave until the discovery of Quinine in the mid-nineteenth century. The mosquito borne disease of malaria killed nearly all white men who ventured fifty miles from its coast and into the interior. Malaria killed large numbers of the native population as well, and with yellow fever, it left them living in the land of the shadow of death. With the discovery of Quinine, exploration and knowledge increased rapidly. Malaria could now be controlled.

Africans also lived in the darkness because of their lack of knowledge of the Christian gospel. All of the tribes in the southern Sudan were pagans with the exception of some Hausa people who were Muslims. The pagans were animistic in their beliefs and worshipped fetishes. A fetish is some inanimate object as simple as a piece of cloth or a stick that is believed to have power and a relationship to the spirit world.

We came to Africa to minister to the overwhelming physical needs of its people, but also to bring the light of the Christian gospel to them.

"The people living in darkness have seen a great light; on those living in the land of the shadow of death a light has dawned." (Matthew 4:16) In the twenty-first century, the majority of Africa's people are now Christians and the center of Christianity has shifted from the Western World to Africa and Asia. Thanks to God's mercy and the efforts of countless missionaries, the light of the gospel now shines over the "Dark Continent."

Harry with Ali Amada and his three wives and children

NEED

*"He who is full loathes honey, but to the hungry
even what is bitter tastes sweet."*

PROVERBS 27:7

The national food of Nigeria has many names among the various tribes. Among the Hausa, it is called "tuwa da miya." As Africans normally eat only two meals a day, it is consumed in the morning and at night. The dish consists of two parts; a ball of pounded yams, guinea corn or rice, and a soup-like sauce into which the starch is dipped. Each individual has a portion of one of the staple starches. A small piece is taken in the fingers and dipped into an individual or common bowl of "miya" or soup. It is then eaten. The miya consists of a base of palm oil seasoned with spices and whatever "greens" are available. Meat, when available, is prized. Okra is a commonly used green. It gives a slimy consistency to the miya. This results in a stringy trail of miya as the fingers are withdrawn from the sauce. Joan and the children loved the food immediately. I suspect the children loved it because they could eat with their fingers. I found it tolerable but far from my favorite. I am not a fan of hot spices, and the slimy, stringy trail of the okra conjured up the image of a spittoon.

One day while visiting outlying villages, I was scheduled to hold a clinic in a Tiv village. I spent the previous night with a Christian Tiv family. Before the families breakfast, I set out early in the morning for the village far to the north. It was a long hot drive and I arrived there around 10:00 a.m. The village was small, but it seemed as if everyone had come to the medical clinic. Several hours later, all had been seen. As I packed up my supplies into the car, I was looking forward to the hospitality of a meal. None was offered.

Africans are famous for their hospitality and always offered a meal even to strangers in their villages. No one had warned me that this village was a known exception. No meal was prepared. Instead, several large yam roots were tossed into the back of my car. I was hungry as I began the long drive back to my host family for the night. I had no way of preparing the yams given to me. I only had the water I had brought along.

I arrived back in the late afternoon. I had not eaten in the past 24 hours as my stomach reminded me. The hosts' wife, with a smile, knew what had happened at the village. She immediately had me sit me down with her husband. It was a most delicious meal of pounded yams with a sauce of palm oil, spices, okra, and goat meat. I felt like, but did not, 'licking the bowl.

"He who is full loathes honey from the comb, but to the hungry even what is bitter tastes sweet." (Proverbs 27:7) Need makes all the difference. How is your devotional life? Do you feed yourself daily with Bible reading and prayer? Or don't you feel the need? We need to daily seek the face of our heavenly Father. Then when storms arise, we can go to Him as a friend not a stranger.

TOUCH FOOD WITH ME

"Who gives food to every creature.
His love endures forever."

PSALM 136:25

Most of us who grew up in North America were reminded by our mothers to clean our plates. We were not to waste food when others in our country or other countries were hungry. In cleaning our plates, we also showed our appreciation for what our mothers had prepared for us. Leaving food could indicate we were not hungry or we did not like what mom had prepared.

Africans are a very hospitable people and most would not think of sending even a stranger from their village hungry. It was an exception to not be offered the hospitality of food. I was often humbled, not only by the offer of food, but by the offering of the best that they had to a relative stranger. America once was more like that when it was small and people were scattered and dependent on the hospitality of strangers.

I quickly learned to appreciate the African custom of, "Ka tabawa abinci da ni;" roughly translated it means, "touch food with me." It was an invitation to share food and if not hungry, to literally only touch it. In Africa cleaning one's plate was an insult to the hostess. It indicated you were not satisfied and had not been given enough to eat. On the other hand, one could only take a bite or two of food and leave the rest and no insult was taken. It merely meant that you were satisfied.

In Africa the men eat first and alone. What they did not eat was then given to the wives and children for their meal. For me, "Ka tabawa abinci da ni", had two great advantages. First of all, I could eat only what I wanted. Often there was food I had never thought of eating or desired to try. I could take a bite and leave the rest without insulting my host or hostess. Secondly, when a portion of meat or an egg appeared on my plate, I could again leave it without insult. Leave it, knowing that the wives and children would gladly eat it and needed it more than I did.

"Who gives food to every creature. His love endures forever." (Psalm 136:25) Neither our culture nor the African one wished to waste food. In Africa the food was left on the plate for others. Here we must learn to take only what we need. Do you take only what you need? Many today are still dependent on the hospitality and generosity of others. Are you hospitable and generous with what you have? Do you gladly share what you do not need with others in greater need?

EQUALITY

*"...I now realize how true it is that God does not
show favoritism but accepts from every nation
the one who fears him and do what is right."*

ACTS 10:34-35

Women in the African culture, as in many cultures, are second-class citizens. In many cases they are present only to work, satisfy their husbands, and provide children, —preferable bearing only male heirs.

The lack of equality is evident every mealtime. At each meal the men are served first. They are given the best of what has been prepared while the women and children are given what is left after the men have eaten. This was vividly demonstrated to me one Sunday when a new missionary on the field. I had just preached my first sermon in the village of Kwambi and was invited to share a meal with the church elders after the service.

My wife, Joan, along with our two children, Christy and Tim, also accompanied me to the village. Ms. Ruth VanderMolen, our neighbor in Takum and a veteran missionary, had also come to hear me preach. We were new to the mission field and just learning and experiencing the many customs of the African culture around us. Ruth had been in the field for over twenty years. She worked diligently as a nurse in preventative medicine. With great effort she crisscrossed this area of the Sudan on foot and bicycle. In numerous villages, she taught the people about sanitation, delivered their babies, and gave immunizations against disease. She was not a stranger to the elders at the Kwambi church. She vigorously protested her exclusion from the meal insisting that the women should also be invited. Her protest was in vain. She and my family were told to wait while I shared a traditional "pastors meal" with the male elders.

All of us carry varying views of women and their roles. Much of this was learned from our family, culture, and experience. It was a great revelation to Peter that God was not a "respecter" of persons. One's wealth, status, birthright, or nationality was insignificant to God. In Galatians 3:28 the Apostle Paul added, "There is neither Jew nor Gentile, slave nor free, nor is there male and female, for you are all one in Jesus Christ." What views do you hold of a women's "place" in the home, business, or in the church? Is it a Biblical view?

DIVORCE

*"Husbands love your wives, just as Christ loved
the church and gave himself up for her."*

EPHESIANS 5:25

Among Nigerian pagans and Muslims few areas of life showed the inequality of women as much as marriage. Pagans were free to take as many as seven wives while Muslims were permitted three.

When I think of marriage in Africa, I think of the popular song, "What has love got to do with it." Unfortunately, the answer was often nothing. A woman was bought for a price determined by her status, beauty, tribal markings, and her father's desires. As many fathers wanted the highest price, eligible young men often could not afford them. Many young women, and even child brides, were sold to much older wealthy males. If a woman was unable to bear children or otherwise displeased her husband, she could be returned to her father for a refund. She was now an outcast and often reduced to prostitution.

Muslims were permitted to have three wives at a time. These women were also bought from their fathers. If she was unsatisfactory to him he merely had to say, "I divorce you" three times, and the woman was sent from his home. For Muslims this was a legal separation. He was now free to take another wife to replace the one he had divorced.

When a woman had children and her husband died, the widow had few rights. Even the children she had borne were the property of her former husbands' brothers or father. The wife owned only the children's love. She could be sent from her home with only the personal gifts her deceased husband had bestowed on her.

The introduction of Christianity is slowly changing the attitudes in this polygamous society. Among the Christians, one wife is now common and widows no longer are sent from their homes, but cared for by loving in-laws.

"Husbands love your wives, just as Christ loved the church and gave himself up for her." (Ephesians 5:25) Unfortunately, the Sudan of Africa is not the only place where husbands do not always love their wives. Divorce has become a worldwide phenomena now affecting nearly one-half of all the marriages in the United States. Formerly "Christian" America is rapidly looking more and more like pagan Africa of sixty years ago. God gave man the privilege of being head of the household. With the privilege came the command that husbands must love their wives. Do you love your wife as Christ loved the church? Christ was willing to give up His life for His bride the Church. Would you? Do you love her enough to die for her?

BARREN

"'The Lord has done this for me', she (Elizabeth)
said. 'In these days he has shown his favor and taken
away my disgrace among the people.'"

LUKE 1:25

God gave woman the privilege of bearing children. As this passage from the scriptures indicates, the inability to do so has long left the childless with feelings of failure and disgrace.

This was certainly true among the African cultures. In a rural agrarian economy, large families produced many workers for the fields. A "good wife" produced many children. She was especially good if she produced male heirs. The African expression, "Namiji ya fi mata" was frequently heard when a child was delivered. A rough translation in English is, "the boy surpasses the girl." Male heirs were always preferred and there was great enthusiasm and joy when they were delivered. In contrast there was little enthusiasm when a little girl was born. I always felt sorry for the mothers as their husband's facial expression and tone of voice expressed their lack of enthusiasm or joy. It was as if they were barren.

Male preference has a long history in many cultures. In India and China female fetuses are often aborted. In countries with royalty, Queens have been replaced because they could not produce a male heir.

The greatest disgrace among the African women, however, was the inability to bear children of either sex. A barren woman not only felt societal disgrace, but it was grounds for divorce. Barren women were often returned to their fathers with a demand for a refund of the bride price.

Children were also a source of social security for women. When their husband died, the deceased husband's brothers or father could send a woman from her home. Grown children, especially, could provide care and sustenance for their mother. Barrenness was a curse.

Barrenness in our society remains a heartache for many women. Some are childless by choice and others through no fault of their own are barren. It is painful for these women when they are asked by others, "How long have you been married now? Isn't it about time you had children"? Be very careful in how you speak to a childless woman. Do not judge or add guilt to her feelings of being unfulfilled.

Harry with Bena Kok and outpatient staff

Loading barge at Katsina Ala river during dry season

GANGRENOUS FETUS

"Why did you bring me out of the womb?
I wish I had died before any eye saw me. If only
I had never come into being, or had been carried
straight from the womb to the grave."

JOB 10:18-19

Without a doubt the worst obstetrical complication I faced in Africa was the presentation of a gangrenous undelivered fetus. The mothers usually arrived at the hospital after many days of unsuccessful labor in the bush. The gangrene was evident by the smell, vaginal discharge, or the protrusion of a gangrenous extremity. The infant had been dead for many hours, usually days.

While a medical student at the University of Michigan, I had been shown old gynecological instruments used to extract a dead fetus. They included a Gigli saw, a sickle, and a pointed scissor used as a cranial trocar. I was assured that in the days of modern medicine, I would never have to use those instruments. I wholeheartedly wished that were true.

As the fetus was now gangrenous, it could not be removed through the abdomen as in a Caesarian section. This would seriously contaminate the mother's abdominal cavity. Subsequently, the infant had to be dissected and removed from below. It was the most unpleasant procedure I have ever performed as a physician.

The mother in these tragic cases did not only lose a child, but suffered the added insult of gangrenous injury to her bladder. In the five cases I attended, all lost more than an entire wall of their bladder. They were now socially unacceptable to their husbands as urine ran constantly down their legs. The huge bladder fistula was impossible for me to repair and there was no one to whom the patient could be referred. Using a technique developed by previous surgeons, the patient's ureters were implanted in the rectum. The rectal sphincter now regulated the flow of urine as well as stool.

It was far from an ideal solution, but the patient was spared from a life as a beggar or a prostitute. In addition, once the urine leakage was corrected, the husbands took their wives back into their homes.

Job said in the bitterness of his soul, ...I wish... I had been carried from the womb straight to the grave." (Job 10:18-19) No one wished that these infants would suffer a similar fate. The lack of medical care brought a tragic ending to these mothers fervent hope to give birth. Are you thankful for the medical care available to you? Do you pray for those still living without medical care where preventable tragedies continue to mar their lives?

CIVIL WAR

"Do not suppose that I have come to bring peace to
the earth. I did not come to bring peace, but a sword.
For I have come to turn "'a man against his father,
a daughter against her mother, a daughter-in-law
against her mother-in-law — a man's enemies will
be the members of his own household.'"

MATTHEW 10:34-36

When we arrived in Nigeria in late summer of 1968, the country had been at civil war for over a year. A year earlier, military officers from the Igbo tribe had assassinated the prime minister of the country. Riots and massacres against those from the Igbo tribe then occurred throughout the country. The coup failed when six months later a counter coup established a federal military government under General Gowen.

Under the threat of beatings and death, ethnic Igbo's fled to their traditional tribal lands in Nigeria's southeast. As these lands included a portion of Nigeria's oil rich delta, it was felt by the Igbo's that a new nation could economically survive. Colonel Ojukwu led the secession of these lands from the federal military government.

The secession led to the war known as the Biafran Civil War to the outside world. It would last for nearly three years. Initially, troops from the federal government pushed the Igbo's back into the land they claimed. There was then a long period of stalemate with loss of life on both sides. Some have estimated over one million deaths occurred. Certainly the majority of those deaths occurred in the breakaway provinces of Biafra. By far, the majority of the deaths were not from fighting, but from starvation. The people in Biafra died when the ports of their tiny country were blockaded and food could only trickle in.

Initially, no new missionaries were allowed into Nigeria after the start of the Civil War. A year later, with the rebels contained in the southeast, we, with other missionaries, were allowed to enter into the country.

"Do not suppose that I have come to bring peace to the earth. I did not come to bring peace, but a sword. [35] For I have come to turn "'a man against his father....." (Matthew 10:34-35) Jesus was of course talking about the consequences of faith in Him. Not all would believe and often it would turn family members against one another. A "Civil War," if you will, between believers and unbelievers. Do you love Jesus? Do you love Him enough to stand against the ridicule or accusations of other members of your family? Many here in Africa are forced to give up everyone they know and love to believe in Christ.

BREATH OF LIFE

*"The Lord God formed a man from the dust of the
ground and breathed into his nostrils the breath
of life, and the man became a living being."*

GENESIS 2:7

Today an African boy about three years old was brought to the outpatient clinic. The mucosal tissue of his eyes and his tongue appeared pale and he was gasping for breath. He was so short of breath that he could not stand, walk, or speak. He appeared at first to be a patient with a severe pneumonia. However, he had no history of fever and his lungs were clear anteriorly and posteriorly to a stethoscopic examination.

A quick examination of a sample of his blood gave an immediate answer. His blood hemoglobin, that portion of the blood that carries oxygen throughout the body, was only 2 grams. It should have been nearly 12 grams. It indicated that 5/6 of his blood had been lost. Although his lungs were normal, the absence of much of the blood's hemoglobin rendered him breathless.

Normally this much blood loss is incompatible with life, but in hookworm disease the blood loss is so slow that the body is often able to compensate to an amazing level. Hookworm disease is common here. It is caused by a microscopic parasite that penetrates through the bare skin, usually through the feet. It can cause severe anemia by blood loss. The parasite is excreted in human waste where it awaits another human host. The African habit of relieving themselves everywhere, including on the walking trails, results in a high incidence of the disease. There is much they need to learn about sanitation and the causes of common diseases.

Our young patient had no audible blood pressure and all of his surface veins had collapsed. A minor surgical procedure called a "cut down" was performed to find a vein for a blood transfusion. The blood was donated by a local high school boy. Before the transfusion was completed there was a dramatic improvement in the child. With an anti-parasitic medication and iron supplements, he would make a quick and complete recovery.

It will take a long time to change customs and understanding, but nurses are educating the populace. Shoes would also decrease the frequency of the disease, but most cannot afford them.

"The Lord God formed a man from the dust of the ground and breathed into his nostrils the breath of life...." (Genesis 2:7) Without it we all die. Do you thank God for even the breaths you take each day? There are many ways your breath can be taken from you. Are you grateful, or do you take breathing and life for granted?

TUBERCULOSIS

"Even though I walk through the valley of the shadow
of death, I will fear no evil, for you are with me;
your rod and your staff, they comfort me."

PSALM 23:4

In the United States tuberculosis is rapidly becoming a disease of the indigent on skid row or those with immune deficiency diseases. Most of the large tuberculosis hospitals are now closed and the disease for most of the population is uncommon. Isolation techniques along with more effective medications and routine TB testing have drastically reduced the number of cases.

In the bush of Africa, however, in the late 1960s, tuberculosis was still rampant. We saw new cases frequently and most were far advanced when they presented at the hospital. We constantly attended thirty or more patients, who were isolated from the other patients, in a small compound a few hundred yards from the main hospital.

Tuberculosis is most commonly spread by small droplets infected with the tubercle bacillus. Coughing, sneezing, and even talking with an infected person is an effective way of transmitting the disease. The communal life style of Africans makes it easy to transmit the disease from person to person. Active disease can take a year or more to fully develop. With active disease, symptoms include shortness of breath, chronic cough, and, for most patients, the loss of a large amount of weight. Their bodies are literally consumed by the disease, hence, an older name for tuberculosis, "Consumption."

Death may be slow with ever increasing weakness, or sudden and dramatic. A few days ago, a thirty-five year old patient presented at the outpatient clinic with severe shortness of breath and cough. A chest x-ray revealed far advanced tuberculosis of both lungs with large tubercular cavities. As I examined him, he had a severe bout of coughing. Suddenly, he began coughing up voluminous amounts of blood as one of the cavities eroded a large blood vessel. There was nothing we could do and he died within minutes.

Each patient was seen at least once a week and more often as necessary. All were given daily tubercular medications for the two months of hospitalization and then sent home with a third month's supply of drugs. Unfortunately, few returned to the hospital for follow up.

"Even though I walk through the valley of the shadow of death, I will fear no evil for thou are with me..." (Psalm 23:4) For three years I was exposed to active TB as I attended numerous patients each week and sometimes daily. Many died, all were seriously ill. Disposable gloves, masks, and gowns, so common today, were unavailable. Yet God protected me! My chest x-ray and TB test have never changed and to this day my TB test remains negative.

GOOD NEWS!

*"How, then, can they call on the one they have
not believed in? And how can they believe in
the one of whom they have not heard?
And how can they hear without someone preaching
to them? And how can they preach unless
they are sent? As it is written: "How beautiful are
the feet of those who bring good news!"*

ROMANS 10:14-15

God is blessing the mission work here in the African Sudan. Many new churches are forming and there is a shortage of trained pastors to care for them. Some African pastors resemble the old circuit-riding ministers of America's early history. They serve a different congregation each Sunday for several weeks before repeating the circuit. It is hard work as they lack transportation other than walking or the use of a bicycle. Some services are then very long as special celebrations such as baptism, confession of faith, and communion must be scheduled on the Sunday when the pastor can be present.

When the pastor is absent, others, including the missionaries, are pressed into service. Some of the missionaries are also pastors. Most are untrained for the ministry. We have been trained as teachers, aircraft pilots, nurses, doctors, carpenters, and administrators.

I come from a family of pastors and at one time struggled with the decision to enter the seminary or medical school. I enjoy preaching and share some of the family's gifts in speaking. The Bible study to prepare a sermon is always enjoyable. The understanding and the truths gained are as beneficial to the one who studies as to the one who hears. Personal Bible study is necessary for each of us to grow and to share our faith.

I often preached once a month. Because of the various languages spoken in our area, I always needed an interpreter in the native churches. Usually one of my surgical assistants would serve as an interpreter for me. Speaking through an interpreter can be disconcerting. Hearing your words translated and spoken in a language you do not understand leaves you with some concerns. Did the interpreter understand what you said? Was he able to accurately convey what you intended?

"...How can they believe in the one of whom they have not heard? ...How beautiful are the feet of them who bring good news." (Romans 10:14-15) Do you have beautiful feet? You need not preach to others, but you must share the good news. Do you study and grow in the Word? You can't share what you do not know. Sharing person to person, friend to friend, is one of the most important means of spreading the good news.

PESTILENCE

"You will not fear the terror of night, nor the arrow that flies by day, nor the pestilence that stalks in the darkness, nor the plague that destroys at midday."

PSALM 91:5-6

In February 1969, our family took a week's vacation in the city of Jos on the plateau. During our brief stay, there was a deep sadness over the mission community. Two nurses from a sister organization died from an unknown disease. Their deaths were strange with a steady deterioration despite the best efforts of those who cared for them.

The first death occurred the week before we came. Ms. Laura Wine had served as a nurse-midwife in a Church of the Brethren mission station in Lassa, Nigeria. It is a tiny village far to the north of Takum, along the Cameroon border. She suddenly became ill with a high fever and only worsened despite medical care. The physician there, in desperation, requested an emergency airlift. The call was answered by our missionary pilot, Ray Browneye, who flew the patient to Jos.[1]

Dr. Jeanette Troup took the patient under her care. Ms. Wine's fever, dehydration, and a strange petechial rash only increased. Before death she showed evidence of severe internal bleeding. She died thirty-six hours after arriving at the hospital. No diagnosis was made, but a viral illness was suspected.

Four days after our arrival in Jos a second nurse, Ms. Charlotte Shaw, also died. She was the nurse who had cared for the first victim of the disease. Her symptoms were identical to those of Ms. Wine. Both nurses followed the same rapid course of deterioration over about ten days. Both nurses despite care had unrelenting fever, throat ulcers, internal hemorrhaging, and a rising white count before their deaths.

Dr. Troup had cared for both patients. She drew a blood sample from both and sent them to Dr. John Frame at the Tropical Medicine Department at Columbia University. He had years earlier initiated a program to investigate deaths from unknown fevers in the tropics. Several deadly viruses, some from Africa and some from South America, were already known. They included Marburg, Argentinian, and Bolivian hemorrhagic fevers. Within a week a third case of the disease would manifest itself.

"You will not the fear the terror of night, nor the arrow that flies by day, ⁶nor the pestilence that stalks in the darkness..." (Psalm 91:5-6) Psalm 91 is that great psalm that speaks of the security found by those that trust in God. Did they not trust enough? No, they trusted completely in God. This time, God in His wisdom gathered His servants to Himself. Like Job, that hedge of protection was removed in God's good time for His good purposes.

¹ John Fuller, *Fever: The hunt for a New Killer Virus* (Grand Rapids, MI: Zondervan, 1974), pg 16-29

SURVIVOR

*"I will not die but live, and will proclaim what
the LORD has done. The LORD has chastened me
severely, but he has not given me over to death."*

PSALM 118:17-18

After returning to Takum, I was informed that Dr. Grey was leaving for the eastern region. He and his wife will be stationed near Lagos and will offer administrative help to a government agency setting up medical clinics in a previous war area.

I cannot say this decision delighted me for it will leave me alone here for two months. There is more than enough work for three, much less attempting it alone. When he returns they will soon leave for another six month furlough. I have accepted it and will pray for health and strength.

Shortly after the Greys arrived in Lagos, they learned that a third nurse, Ms. Penny Pinneo, had just arrived on a flight from Jos. She was deathly ill with the same symptoms as those of the two other nurses who had died at the hospital there. Penny had in fact also cared for both of her colleagues. When she became ill, Dr. Troup had decided to not only send blood samples, but also the patient to Dr. Frame in New York.

Penny was placed in the Pest House outside the city of Lagos as the University Hospital refused her admission. The Pest House was a crude rundown facility for the care of tribesman with various contagious diseases. Bea Grey quickly volunteered to share her nursing care with Dorothy Davis, the nurse who had accompanied her from Jos. Dr. Stanley Foster, an American Public Health physician, agreed to supervise her care.[2]

Two days later this critically ill American nurse was placed on a Pan Am flight to New York City. There, Dr. Frame awaited her arrival and would admit her to an isolation room in Columbia Presbyterian Hospital. Penny struggled for life, and for many days it appeared she would also die. Then ever so slowly she began to improve; the first survivor in this outbreak of an as yet unknown disease and without any known treatment.

In the bush at Takum, it took months for even this information to arrive. Along with the already known deadly diseases around us we now had a new one; an unknown disease that quickly killed both its victims and those who cared for them. Where did it come from? How was it transmitted? What or who harbored it?

Penny eventually had a miraculous recovery as her immune system defeated the disease. She could certainly say, "I will not die but live, and will proclaim what the LORD has done. The LORD has chastened me severely, but he has not given me over to death." Psalm 11:17-18

[2] John Fuller, *Fever* (Grand Rapids, MI: Zondervan, 1974), pg 62

TOO DEADLY

"For the life of the creature is in the blood,
and I have given it to you to make atonement
for yourselves on the altar; it is the blood
that makes atonement for one's life."

LEVITICUS 17:11

The medical communities joy over Penny Pineo's survival from Lassa fever was short lived. Soon it was shocked again by the onset of the disease in one of the virologist who was studying it. Dr. Jordi Casals, one of the virologists at the Yale arbovirus laboratory, was the next non-African victim of the disease. He had been extremely careful as he continued his studies of the deadly virus. However, a small mistake in handling the virus one day was all that was needed to infect him.

He rapidly became severely ill as all of the others had done. His fever was unrelenting with the same rash, sore throat and signs of bleeding. Despite the care of his colleagues his death appeared eminent. Dr. Casal's life now hung in the balance. There had previously been three known non-African cases of the disease and only one had survived.

Meanwhile, Dr. Casals colleagues struggled with a difficult decision. His condition continued to deteriorate and without treatment he would surely die. There was no treatment except the possibility of a blood transfusion from Penny Pineo who had developed antibodies to the disease in her survival. The recipents reaction to this transfusion was unknown.

Penny was more than willing to donate her blood and faced with Dr. Casals death, his colleagues decided to try the blood transfusion. The blood was soon transfused into his body. Slowly his symptoms improved as the antibodies that had saved her life did the same for him. [3]

News of the deadly virus was slow to reach the outside world and the virus studies continued with renewed care at the Yale arborvirus laboratory. Soon yet another death from the virus would end all further study at Yale. A headline in the New York times would then proclaim, "New Fever Virus so Deadly That Research Halts." [4]

Information about the disease was even slower in reaching us in the bush of Africa. There were many rumors as well as facts about the course of the disease. There had been many more cases at the hospital in Jos, but more survived than died and the epidemic seemed to have passed.

"...The life of the creature is in the blood... Lev. 17:11 This passage from the book of Leviticus was the reason given to Israel prohibiting their eating the blood of animals. For Dr. Casals, his life was in the blood transfusion from Penny Pineo in the form of antibodies against the virus.

[3] John Fuller, *Fever* (Grand Rapids, MI: Zondervan,1974) pg. 143

[4] John fuller, *Fever* (Grand Rapids, MI: Zondervan, 1974), pg. 173

UNKNOWN

"Show me O Lord my life's end and the number
of my days; let me know how fleeting is my life."

PSALM 39:4

At the Columbia Presbyterian hospital, Dr. Frame continued his research and study of the largely unknown disease. There were now four non-African victims of the disease and two had survived. The virus was given the name Lassa after the small village in Africa from which the first victim had come. It appeared related to a family of viruses that caused South American hemorrhagic fevers.

Under strict isolation procedures the study continued at the Yale arbovirus laboratory. Access to the laboratory where the virus was studied was strictly limited. Only a few virologists were allowed to conduct experiments with the virus. Each was keenly aware that they were dealing with death; a death only seen with an electron microscope.

Then tragedy struck again. A laboratory technician, Juan Roman, working in another laboratory suddenly became ill. Initially it was felt he was suffering from Typhus. Investigation revealed that he had no contact with the Lassa virus and was in fact working on a totally unrelated project. Over several days his condition worsened following the same deterioration as the victims of Lassa fever. Despite the best supportive care he died a few days later. After his death the cultures revealed he too had died of Lassa fever.[5]

The technician's death only added to the fear of the new disease. How could it possibly have been transmitted to Juan Romans? Immediately all research at Yale was halted.[6] All studies and specimens were now sent to the new CDC laboratory in Atlanta, Georgia. There were no new cases in Jos and as yet we have seen no cases at the Takum or Mkar hospitals. The epidemic seems to have passed.

"Show me O Lord, my life's end and the number of my days." Do you know when you will die? Although we all know that someday we will die, the number of our days is unknown. Are you prepared to meet God or do you think you will be able to prepare at some later time? Like Juan Romans your life may end suddenly and without warning. Are you ready?

[5] John Fuller, *Fever* (Grand Rapids, MI: Zondervan, 1974) pg. 171-172

[6] John Fuller, *Fever* (Grand Rapids, MI: Zondervan, 1974) pg. 172

CONQUEROR

"Yet for your sake we face death all day long;
we are considered as sheep to be slaughtered."

PSALM 44:22

Nearly a year later, in January of 1970, our focus on Lassa fever was suddenly sharpened once again. It was announced on the mission radio that Dr. Jeanette Troup had died of suspected Lassa fever in the hospital in Jos.

Once again a deep sadness settled over the mission community over her sudden death. Lassa had once again claimed another missionary victim. Most of us in the medical community knew Dr. Troup, as did Joan and I. I had consulted with her on a few occasions and she had examined Joan at the onset of her third pregnancy.

We later learned that Dr. Troup cut herself during an autopsy on an African patient. This patient was suspected of having Lassa fever. During the previous two weeks, fourteen new patients had been admitted to the Evangel Hospital in Jos; twelve of them had a similar illness and four had died. As before, Dr. Troup had collected blood samples from all of them. They were now sent to the Virus Laboratory at the

University of Ibadan, located in Ibadan, Nigeria. Since the onset of the new disease and the studies at Columbia they had been equipped to handle and test for the Lassa virus. Later it was confirmed that all fourteen of these patients had Lassa fever.

Like the previous deaths from the disease, Dr. Troup died in about ten days. Her illness followed the same deadly course—unrelenting fevers, sore throat, rash, and terminal internal bleeding. Much later it was learned that Dr. Casals had sent bottles of blood containing the antibodies to the virus to Dr. Troup.[7] It was hoped she could use them to spare others lives. Unfortunately, they did not arrive in time to spare hers.

In the bush at Takum and at our other hospital at Mkar, no known cases of the hemorrhagic fever had been seen. Little was yet known about the disease, its hosts, or its transmission. In the bush we had as yet not seen Lassa fever and thanked God for sparing us and those we cared for.

"...For your sake we face death all day long..." (Psalm 44:22) The psalmist laments to God that because of Israel's relationship to Him they were oppressed by the nations around them. Later the Apostle Paul quotes these words to remind Christians that nothing can separate us from God's love. Dr. Troup's love for God put her as a missionary physician at the front of a battle against a deadly new disease. Yet she knew and we know that nothing, even death, can separate us from Him.

[7]   John G. Fuller, *Fever* (Grand Rapids, MI: Zondervan, 1974), pg 202-205

BLOOD

*"See now that I am he! There is no god beside me.
I put to death and I bring to life, I have wounded and
I will heal, and no one can deliver out of my hand."*

DEUTERONOMY 32:39

Our bush hospital does not have a blood bank, and patients seeking elective major surgery must bring three relatives with them willing to donate blood. In emergency situations, we seek volunteers among the students at the mission high school. One specific emergency, ruptured ectopic pregnancies, often immediately requires a large amount of blood. Out of necessity we will then auto transfuse the patients own blood.

Most of the patients with an ectopic pregnancy are no longer actively bleeding by the time they are seen. Most are in shock from the lost of blood into their abdominal cavity. The low blood pressure coupled with the pressure of the blood in the abdomen has stopped most of the internal bleeding. However, anywhere from 5 to 8 pints of blood are now free inside their abdominal cavity.

We begin by starting an IV of fluid in each arm to replace some of the fluid volume of the blood loss. As soon as the surgical excision is made, the bleeding will resume as the pressure inside the abdomen is released. An immediate attempt to control the ruptured blood vessels was then accomplished with a clamp or the pressure from a free hand. The blood filling the cavity was then removed with a small sterile cup. It was then poured through a lab filter into a sterile bottle containing sodium citrate. The filter removes any clotted blood. The sodium citrate keeps the recovered blood from further clotting and adds bicarbonate to the blood.

Once a bottle has been filled, it quickly replaces one of the IVs. Our most recent patient a week ago, received six units of her own blood recovered from her abdomen. The most I have recovered was eight units. This unique form of blood replacement was useful at least twenty times over two-and-a-half years. All of the patients survived while none had a serious reaction to the transfusion of their recovered blood. Without the blood, several might have died and all would have had a prolonged recovery.

"...There is no God beside me. I put to death and I bring to life..." (Deuteronomy 32:39) Sometimes doctors are accused of playing god. But only God can give life. Physicians may, by His grace, preserve or extend it for a while, but they cannot give it. On what or whom do you depend for your life? The Bible is clear. Life and death are only in the hands of a sovereign God. Do you know Him?

BARRELS

*"At the present time your plenty will supply
what they need, so in turn their plenty
will supply what you need..."*

2 CORINTHIANS 8:14

We finally received some good news from the Palm Shipping Lines. The thirteen barrels, we shipped late last summer, have finally arrived in Lagos. When we shipped them in August 1968, we expected them in about three months, but it took nearly eight. During this time we had to borrow extensively from our mission friends. We felt embarrassed, but all were kind and generous. Joan especially wearied of asking for yet something else when there was plenty in our missing barrels.

Monday, our barrels arrived aboard the mission lorry as it returned from Lagos. Joan tore into the barrels and emptied them one after another. She emptied four in no time flat and the house was littered with all the things that would have to be put away. She soon realized, as exciting as it was, we had better absorb and begin storing things before emptying any more.

One of the barrels contained a little Red Flyer wagon. Christy and Tim met me at the door with its handle in their hands. It was clear that Dad was not permitted to look any further in the barrels until the wheels and handle had been put on. They are now busy pulling it around the compound and visiting all our neighbors. They are proud as punch of their new toy, although occasionally arguing about whose turn it was to pull it.

The empty barrels came in handy as well. We used several to store our perishable foods and to keep, at least the visible, insects and pests away. It felt good to put the 100 pounds of flour into one of the barrels. That eliminated at least the problem with the mice, but not the problem of the weevils already in the flour. We didn't need all of the barrels and shared the majority of the them with others, including our two houseboys. Their mud huts lacked much of the protection that was in our home. A sturdy steel barrel with a lid was a godsend to protect their food from mice, rats, snakes, and other creatures.

Even the mattress we shipped had arrived in its crate intact. Now we can have a local carpenter make a frame for it. Then we will hang the new mosquito netting we purchased from England many months ago. Our mattress had no apparent water damage or stains. Other missionaries were not as fortunate with many horror stories of mold and water stains on their mattresses.

At last we could return all that we had borrowed and now lend to others. It is truly easier to give than to receive. "At the present time your plenty will supply what they need, so in turn their plenty will supply what you need..." (2 Corinthians 8:14) The Apostle Paul's admonition was that Christians should share with each other so that no one had too much and no one lacked anything. Do you have and know that others lack?

THE GENERAL

*"This is also why you pay taxes, for the authorities
are God's servants, who give their full time to
governing. Give to everyone what you owe them:
If you owe taxes, pay taxes; if revenue, then revenue;
if respect, then respect; if honor, then honor."*

ROMANS 13:6-7

Nigeria was ruled by a military government. General
Gowen was the head of state and General Gomwalk
was the governor of our individual state. Monday, we were
informed by radio, that the general would be inspecting our
hospital on Wednesday. He also requested that he would like
to share a noon meal with us.

Our head nurse, Mae Mast, scampered to get the hospital
clean. She always kept the hospital clean, but she wanted it
especially so for the general. Harold Padding and his wife, Vi,
agreed to host the dinner in their home.

The general's entourage was impressive. To get to Takum
from the north one had to cross the Katsina Ala River fifty miles
from our village. There was no bridge over the river which was
over a half-mile wide. Automobiles were brought over on a

raft-like barge, one or two at a time, along with some of the passengers. It must have been quite a sight. I am sure that this bush crossing, at the end of a narrow two-track dirt road, had not seen many BMW's before. Especially, vehicles accompanied by a general and soldiers with automatic weapons.

The general, with his entourage, arrived at the hospital in mid-morning along with the many luxury vehicles and trucks. The general was also accompanied by many district officers, commissioners, tribal chiefs, as well as gun-toting soldiers, and policemen. General Gomwalk, in full military dress, stepped out of the first vehicle and warmly greeted us. He had been educated in mission schools and spoke excellent English. He and I toured the hospital together. He showed a genuine interest in the people there, workers as well as patients. He made a special effort to shake hands with many of the staff members and some of the patients. A visit we had anticipated with some anxiety went very well and was very enjoyable.

After finishing our tour of the hospital, we adjourned to the Padding's home. Joan along with several other missionaries and their wives joined us there. Several guests accompanied the general. The conversation was friendly and animated and from all appearances the general enjoyed his visit. Soon after dinner, he and his entourage departed. It had been a very good day, however, one in which I accomplished very little medically.

"This is why you pay taxes, for the authorities are God's servants, who give their full time to governing. [7]Give everyone what you owe them..." (Romans 13:6-7) Do you respect and honor those in authority over you? Do you respect them even if they belong to a different political party? There is no authority but that given by God.

NEW ADDITION

"Sons are a heritage from the LORD,
children a reward from him."

PSALM 127:3

When we came to Africa eight months ago, we had two small children and Joan was unsure if she were ready to have a baby here in the African bush. She had been on birth control since she quit nursing our son, Tim, after his first birthday. He was now nearly three. Previously, we had decided that we would wait until after I completed my military service before considering our third child. Joan's earlier experiences with poisonous snakes, did not relieve her anxiety, especially, about bringing another child into this situation. However, as the months went by, she became more and more comfortable with the idea of a new addition. She saw several other missionaries give birth here and now was no longer afraid.

We did not plan this pregnancy. After experiencing some difficulties with her birth control pills, Joan took the advice of a visiting Australian gynecologist. She decided to stop her pills for a few months. This month she missed her period and has all the familiar symptoms of her previous pregnancies. It appears we will be expecting our third child in November 1969.

Several other missionary wives are also expecting a child during the months of October through December. There should be five new additions to the mission family. Normally, the ladies are sent for delivery to the city of Jos about six weeks before their due date. None of the couples look forward to this separation, but the larger city has better facilities and far more personnel, including doctors and nurses.

The recent deaths of the two nurses in Jos and the fulminating illness of a third has added a whole new dimension to our normal routine. The idea of sending healthy expectant mothers to a hospital where there have been unexplained deaths did not seem very wise. I am leaning very heavily toward delivering all of the women here in the bush.

Delivering the women here also has its drawbacks. I will be alone as the Greys will be on furlough. With no backup to consult, no blood bank, and limited facilities, I am sure my anxiety level will rise. Finally, this meant I would also deliver my own child as well. While a pleasant thought, physicians usually find others to care for their own family. Being emotionally attached to the patient can be problematic, especially if there are complications. I will pray for quick and normal deliveries.

"Sons are a heritage from the LORD, children a reward from Him." (Psalm 127:3) In the Old Testament, sons were a heritage because without a son there was no inheritance in the promise land. But all children are a gift from God. Not an accident, not a sign of virility or fertility, but a gift from God. Accept and love them as a sign of His favor.

GOD'S FREE PSYCHIATRIST

*"For physical training is of some value, but godliness
has value for all things, holding promise
for both the present life and the life to come."*

1 TIMOTHY 4:8

I have felt extremely tired for the past few weeks. The hospital remains very busy and its responsibility lies entirely on my shoulders. Despite hundreds of major surgical cases, I am amazed how frequently I still see something new. It is not unusual for me to take a surgical text or anatomy book with me to the operating theatre.

Lately, I had been concerned about my fatigue and weight loss. I have lost nearly thirty pounds since arriving, and it is especially noticeable in my clothing. I have already punched new holes into my belt to keep my shorts from falling down. My clothes increasingly appear to be hand-me-downs from an older, bigger brother.

A frequent Hausa greeting is "Ina aiki" or how is your work? The standard reply is "Aiki da gadiya" or I am grateful to God for it. I am grateful and count it a privilege to be serving my brothers and sisters here. Smiling has always been easy for me, but at times lately, it is difficult to keep the stress out of my voice.

Two weeks ago, I joined the Takum Tennis Club. The facilities are simple, consisting only of a thin, cracked, concrete court located in a vacant lot. The membership is made up primarily of the male nurses from the hospital and a few other tradesmen and school teachers. Each member had varying levels of skill, but almost all were athletic and very competitive.

I would never have imagined how therapeutic tennis would be. I was so tired when I arrived two weeks ago, I didn't think I could lift my tennis racket above my head. However, after playing for an hour in over a 100-degree heat, I was amazed to find that I felt like a new man. My energy had returned and I was ready to tackle the hospital work again. It soon dawned on me that the fatigue and exhaustion were mostly a result of the mental stress and pressures at the hospital. My problem was as much mental as physical.

This new pearl of wisdom I have since passed on to thousands of my patients. Exercise is God's free psychiatrist! Try it before pills and other medication when fatigued and stressed. It is amazing how many solutions pop into your head when you temporarily forget about the problems stressing you. As far as my weight loss, it could easily be explained by my high level of activity and the decreased amounts of food I ate here.

"For physical training is of some value, but godliness has value in all things..." (I Timothy 4:8) Do you feel tired, overburdened, and stressed? Certainly practice godliness first! Have an active prayer life and Bible study. But remember, you are body and soul. Exercise strengthens the body and exercise can relieve the stresses and daily pressures of life.

BABEL

"That is why it was called Babel—because there the
LORD confused the language of the whole world.
From there the LORD scattered them over
the face of the whole earth."

GENESIS 11:9

The Greys returned from Lagos and will be leaving for their furlough in six weeks. Herm said he hadn't treated a patient since he left two months ago. That will be easy to remedy because he can start rounds tomorrow.

The executive committee on the field had made it official that I will not be receiving any formal language training. There simply wasn't time. Once the Grey's leave, I will be alone for the rest of this year. Since my arrival, the press of hospital work and the shortage of physicians has prevented my language training. Most of the other missionaries were able to leave for a few months and concentrate on formal language education, but for me that has been impossible.

Hausa is most commonly spoken here and is the trade language of this West African country. Those educated have varying English skills, but most speak only their native tongue. A review of our patients showed that as many as twenty-five language groups come here for treatment. Patients from the Tiv, Kuteb, and Jukun tribes represented the vast majority and, hence, would be the language skills most needed.

Making rounds in the hospital each day can certainly be like Babel. Usually two or three nurses, each of whom spoke two or more tribal languages, accompanied me. Occasionally, even then, there were patients whose language was not spoken by anyone here. We then treated the patient based on my clinical and physical examination. Usually, within a day or two, we found someone who could speak to them.

I continued to learn basic greetings and various other medical words. It is amazing what even poor attempts at speaking does for patient rapport. Especially, if the attempts were made in a good humor, with a pleasant smile, and sincerely. A broad smile has a universal meaning in any language.

Without language, however, it does make the patient/ physician relationship much less satisfying. I have always enjoyed the verbal interaction with my patients. Any deeper relationship requires language. I also enjoyed verbalizing my faith, and without language this is nearly impossible other than by the attitude and kindnesses shown.

"...There the Lord confused the language of the whole world..." (Genesis 11:9) Do you share your faith? Do you speak their language? Increasingly, speaking to others, even in our own cultures, sometimes seems like Babel. Cultural mores and Biblical truths once were common even among the unchurched. Today speaking to many seems as if you are speaking in a foreign language. Pray for understanding and the words to say.

HIGH PLACES

"The high places, however, were not removed;
the people continued to offer sacrifices
and burn incense there."

2 KINGS 12:3

Normally, one of the physicians will visit outlying clinics scattered in the villages many miles from Takum. This had not been done for some time because of the doctor shortage. Dr. Grey suggested I make a few of those visits before he left.

Today, I am flying to the village of Bete with one of our hospital staff. Yahubu Bete works in our outpatient pharmacy and has been a Christian for a long time. He was born in the village fifty years ago, and his brother is the village chief. About a thousand people now live there. Bete is thirty miles from Takum and can be reached only on foot or by plane.

The village lies at the base of a beautiful high mountain. Multiple tall rocky spires rise from its summit easily identifying the mountain. I could not help but think of the many Biblical passages that referred to the high places. Places used primarily for pagan worship, but also for worship of Jehovah.

Bete was once a pagan village. Its inhabitants lived high on the mountain for their own protection from slave-trading tribes. Yakubu pointed up at one of the four spires high on the mountain. "I was born there at the base of that spire," he said. He was a little boy of four or five when the villagers came off of the mountain in 1922. British law had now been established in Nigeria and the villagers were encouraged to live on the plains under their protection.

I visited with the local Nigerian medical attendant and saw several patients with him. The attendants have a few simple medications primarily used to treat burns, malaria, and worm infestations. They are also instructed in the care of wounds and snake bites. Two of the patients we saw appeared very ill. One was vomiting up blood and had either an ulcer or a more serious stomach cancer. The other had a hard mass on the right side of his abdomen, which felt suspiciously like a cancer of the liver. Both made the return flight to Takum with us for further care and investigation.

"The high places, however, were not removed; the people continued to offer sacrifices and burn incense there." (2 Kings 12:3) People in America think the high places are for base jumping and skiing. Yet at no previous time have so many worshipped false gods and idols. Stadiums are filled on Sundays while millions seek the gods of pleasure and leisure in a hundred different ways. Yet church attendance decreases and Christianity is ridiculed. Who or what do you worship?

SAFETY

*"I will lie down and sleep in peace, for you alone,
O LORD make me dwell in safety."*

PSALM 4:8

We are reminded each day of our dependence on God for safety. Here in the bush of Africa, we never felt in control of our circumstances or environment. There was so little we could control or even anticipate.

Traveling the "roads" between the many villages was a good example. One recent weekend, the whole family accompanied me as we visited outpatient clinics. We borrowed the mission's station wagon and set out early one morning. The children were excited about the trip and like children everywhere wondered, "Are we just about there."

Traveling the dirt roads of Africa is hot and dusty. Even with the car windows closed, dust seemed to find an infinite number of ways to enter the car. However, if the windows were not open, the heat was nearly unbearable. The road twisted and turned among tall grasses with many blind curves. In many places, the road was only two deep grooves with a high center between them. Much of the time, to protect the undercarriage of the car, we rode with one tire in a groove and the other riding the high center of the road. The roads were rutted with rocks and holes and very hard on the suspension. Twenty miles an hour was high speed, and it was difficult to feel safe and comfortable. One never knew when a large lorry would suddenly appear around a blind curve and take over the road. The lorries were usually driven very fast and often by young drivers who could barely see over the windshield. There were few rules of the road; however, whoever was bigger usually had the right of way.

When travel was coupled with the fact that there were no gas stations, motels, or phone booths, one realizes how dependent we were on God for safe travel. Especially since tire repairs and mechanical problems were yours to solve, whether you were a mechanic or not. Add pedestrians, livestock, wild animals, and cattle herds and you realize why we never traveled without many a prayer for safety.

"I will lie down and sleep in peace, for you alone, O LORD make me dwell in safety." (Psalm 4:8) Sleeping or awake we are dependent on God for safety. Do you pray for safety when you drive each day? Or do you feel in control of the circumstances and your environment? Unfortunately, in familiar surroundings we often feel independent of God. Rest assured, you are as dependent as we were in the bush of Africa. It's your perception that is in error.

FAREWELL

"...Well done good and faithful servant!
You have been faithful with a few things;
I will put you in charge of many things.
Come and share your master's happiness."

MATTHEW 25:23

Last night we had a farewell party for Rev. Edward and Nell Smith. They are retiring to the United States after nearly forty years of service here in Nigeria. Reverend Smith was initially loaned from the British branch of the Sudan United Mission to serve with the infant Christian Reformed Mission work in Nigeria. Rev. Ed Smith later married Nell Breen in the early 1930s and both have served since that time with Christian Reformed World Missions.

For the past few weeks, the Smiths had been saying goodbye to numerous churches, fellow missionaries, and African friends with whom they had worked for so many years. No doubt their feelings are bittersweet. They have been with the mission since its early beginnings. Now they were saying goodbye to their life's work. They were here with the first few mission converts and now were saying goodbye to a thriving African church that outnumbered its parent in the United States.

After dinner, Ed and Nell regaled us with stories as they reminisced about their years in Africa. We felt that we were living quite primitively, but our experience was nothing compared to how they began. They lived in a native hut and their movements were limited to how far they could walk or bicycle in a day. We shipped out many barrels, while they rarely shipped out more than a barrel of flour and a barrel of sugar. Fortunately, by the time of their arrival, the medicine, Quinine, had been discovered. It was the first effective treatment for malaria. The disease that had given Africa the reputation as the white man's grave could now be controlled. Missionaries could now live in the African interior.

The Smiths will leave Africa in a few days, quite possibly, for the last time. No doubt they will deeply miss their adopted country and the African people with whom they had worked for a lifetime.

"…Well done good and faithful servant(s)! You have been faithful with a few things; I will put you in charge of many things. Come and share your master's happiness." Matthew 25:23) What will the Master say to you? The point of the parable is not to just play it safe while we wait for Christ's coming again. We are to be working and producing fruit for the Kingdom. Are you working? Are you bearing the fruit Christ chose you to produce?

EMERGENCY

"...This is a day of distress and rebuke and disgrace,
as when children come to the moment of birth and
there is no strength to deliver them."

ISAIAH 37:3

The afternoon radio broadcast brought a call for help from a mission station over 100 miles to the south at Serti. It was from the midwife, alone at the station as the missionaries were on vacation. She called because one of her patients had been in labor for over thirty-six hours and was unable to deliver. She pleaded for an emergency C-section if at all possible.

It was already past mid-afternoon, but the pilot felt there was still enough time. We would, however, have to spend the night in Serti. I raced to the hospital to pick up a sterile surgical pack and then went straight to the airfield on my motorcycle. The aircraft was already warming up and in a few minutes we were on our way to Serti.

Upon arrival, the midwife led me to a small building that served as a maternity center and delivery room. Sunlight was slowly failing, and the room was lit only by two small windows and a kerosene lantern. An examination of the young women found her totally exhausted. Intermittently, she cried out with labor pains before falling back to sleep. A pelvic exam revealed a completely dilated cervix but the fetal head was high and unengaged. The infant's heart tones, however, were strong and regular.

It was too dark to do the C-section in the building so we carried a long wooden table outside. This would be my first C-section under local anesthesia and without a surgical assistant. The midwife had already started an IV. I did a quick surgical prep and draped her with the sterile towels and drapes we had brought. Through the midwife, I explained to the patient what I would be doing. We then prayed together for her strength and my skill to perform the operation.

We began by infiltrating the skin for incision. Deeper tissues would be infiltrated with local anesthesia as I reached them. As there was only a local effect from the anesthesia, the patient will tell you if the tissue is not anesthetized. I quickly entered the abdomen, opened the uterus, and delivered a healthy infant. Sunlight was of little help, and if it were not for the flashlight held above the wound, surgery would have been impossible.

This above quote of King Hezekiah ended in joy as God showed His strength and delivered Jerusalem from Sennacherib. The mother and child's day of distress also became a day of joy as we were able to reach them. How big is your God? Do you trust him to deliver you?

GROUNDED

"God is our refuge and strength, an ever-present
help in trouble. Therefore we will not fear,
though the earth give way and the mountains
fall into the heart of the sea."

PSALM 46:1-2

The Nigerian government had just issued an order grounding all of the mission aircraft. Since the war began, the mission pilots were required to give twenty-four hour notice of their flights. The flights were then authorized. Now, no flights would be permitted even with notification.

Apparently, there had been a setback for the Nigerian military forces in its war against Biafra. Someone taught the rebels how to arm small civilian aircraft. These planes were similar in size to the mission aircraft. Armed with rockets and machine guns, the rebel planes have been strafing areas controlled by the federal government. Our pilots were told that several MiG fighters and a bomber of the Nigerian Air Force have been destroyed on the ground. The government has responded by grounding all small aircraft. All planes of this size would be shot down. Commercial flights were not affected. How long this ban would remain in effect was unknown.

We soon felt the effects of this government order. Airplanes have been our lifeblood isolated here in the bush. Road trips are difficult and dependent on the conditions of the road. It has been a very heavy rainy season, making the roads often impassable. There is little or no road maintenance except that which is done by hand and shovel. There would be no more emergency patient flights, and the mail, which had been regular every two weeks, would now become very irregular.

The mail will now have to come from Jos by car. That is, whenever a vehicle is able make the trip. At present the Katsina Ala River is flooded a half-mile beyond its banks. This makes the crossing there iffy as the barge cannot always get to the wet season crossing. The river must be crossed if one is to get to Takum from the north.

"God is our refuge and strength, an ever-present help in trouble..." (Psalm 46:1-2) Why does God allow adversity? Why are Christians' lives not smooth and free of trouble? Perhaps because we, His children, think we are self-reliant when life is going well. Perhaps because we believe we can handle life. Adversity is a sharp reminder of who is in control and where our refuge, strength, and help must come from.

ANGELS

"For he will command his angels concerning
you to guard you in all your ways."

PSALM 91:11

We have tickets on a commercial flight from Jos to Lagos this week Saturday. We will be visiting our friends from our days in the air force. We are driving to Jos since the airplanes have been grounded. Hopefully, we will be able to take a barge across the Katsina Ala River. The river is now at flood stage, and the last we heard the barge was under repair. We won't know if it is fixed until we get there. If it is repaired, we will be able to cross the river and make it to Makurdi before nightfall. There we will stay with the DeGroot family and be half-way to Jos. The trip to Makurdi went smoothly. The barge had been repaired, and we were able to use the wet season crossing. We were only delayed a few hours at the river. Nevertheless, we were delighted to see the familiar faces of the Degroot's and for a hot meal and a bed. We started out early the next morning for Jos.

There is little past the city of Makurdi, only tiny bush villages and tribes with strange languages. The countryside was increasingly hilly with only a few trees and grass. As we approached the crest of a particularly long and steep hill, the Volkswagen Beetle suddenly stopped. I quickly put my foot on the brakes and glanced in the rear view mirror. There was no other traffic, only the steep descent behind us. I let the car roll back down the hill and parked under a lone tree at the side of the road.

I opened up the boot (trunk) of the car and saw the engine covered with a thick red coat of dust just like the car's exterior. The sudden stop seemed electrical, but I didn't see the problem. The only other traffic was a large lorry which raced down the hill in the opposite direction. Its cargo space was packed with Nigerians holding on for dear life. No one even glanced at us. While Joan comforted the children and gave them a drink of water, I stepped away from the car and stood under the tree. I offered a short prayer, "Lord we have a problem and I don't know what to do. I need someone with mechanical knowledge and tools. And Lord if he could speak English that would be a big help."

No other traffic passed. However, within fifteen minutes of my prayer a covered pick-up truck crested the hill and then stopped alongside us. "Cheerio mate what seems to be the problem?" the driver asked. He briefly checked the vehicle and then opened the back of his truck. I never have seen more tools. After a few minutes of brushing away the dust, he found a loose distributer wire. "Here is your problem mate." Within minutes the wire was reattached. He refused remuneration other than our profuse thanks. As we approached the crest of the hill a second time, I reflected on my short prayer. In the middle of literally nowhere, without a telephone, during a civil war, a service call in fifteen minutes and in "English" as requested.

"For he will command his angels concerning you to guard you in all your ways." Psalm 91:11

FRIENDS

"A man of many companions may come to ruin,
but there is a friend who sticks closer than a brother."

PROVERBS 18:24

The commercial flight from Jos to Lagos Saturday morning was uneventful. It was, however, a bit unnerving clearing security at the Lagos airport. There were armed soldiers everywhere and in far greater number than we had ever seen. We were briefly questioned and released. Outside the terminal, a driver from the American Embassy was waiting to chauffeur us to the Langley's home.

Colonel John Langley was the military attaché to the country of Nigeria. He and his wife, Emily, had been in country for nearly a year. Over a year before, I had met them in my flight surgeon's office at Andrews Air Force Base. They had learned that I was going as a medical missionary to Nigeria while John was waiting for his appointment as the military attaché. We hit it off immediately, and they promised to get in touch with us when we both were in the country.

They lived in a beautiful two-story home near the ocean in Lagos. We were given the entire upstairs of that home, except for the bedrooms of their two older children. It was beyond our wildest dreams. Emily was a gracious hostess and soon won over both children by bringing them to play with the toys their children had collected. With both chef and household help, we felt we were in a palace.

John and Emily had grown up in a small town in Kansas. They were the kind of people we had grown up with. They were also Christians. We instantly renewed our friendship and after dinner each night would sit for hours just chatting together. Joan was delighted with their air conditioning after enduring the 108 degree heat in the bush. She was now five months pregnant. She was also happy to be able to play a piano once again. Neither John nor his wife played. John loved to hear the piano and nightly asked Joan to play before we all retired.

We could not have been more relaxed or enjoyed each other's company more. After nearly a year of hospital work, it was a welcome break. It was a wonderful time to relax and prepare for the long six months of work ahead of us.

"...a man of many companions may come to ruin, but there is a friend who sticks closer than a brother." (Proverbs 18:24) The Biblical admonition is a warning to be careful in selecting our friendships. Some may bring ruin while others are just like family. What kind of friends do you have? Where are they leading you?

SLAVERY

"Masters, provide your slaves with what is right
and fair, because you know that you also
have a Master in heaven."

COLOSSIANS 4:1

One day, John, Emily, and their teenagers, took all of us to the beach along the Atlantic Ocean. Small wooden fishing boats, their nets drying in the sun, were scattered along the beach. Some of the boats were smaller and narrower than a row boat. Others were considerably larger and anchored in the surf. All of the smaller boats had outriggers to stabilize them. The water was warm, and the waves allowed us to surf with boogie boards.

For us the beach was a delightful treat. However, this area, in the not too distant past, was used in the slave trade. It is still known on some of the maps of Africa as the "slave coast." It was here that the slave traders brought captive tribal peoples to be sold abroad on the slave ships of England, France, and the Netherlands.

When the English Parliament abolished slavery in their colonies in 1807, the English placed warships along this coast. Their task was to intercept the slave ships of other nations and return the people to Africa. It took a long time, and as recently as World War I, the French were still taking Africans to the trenches of Europe.

It is hard to believe or understand that today more people are in slavery than at any other time in human history. One would think by now that slavery would have been abolished. Yet the news is filled with reports of human trafficking. Countless human beings are still being transported internationally and sold in the sex trade or for domestic servants. Most are from poor and economically deprived third world countries. Others are taken captive in modern western societies.

The Bible doesn't forbid slavery, but in Colossians, masters are told to provide their slaves with what is right and fair. Is there anything more right or fair than a slave's freedom? Wherever Christianity has been preached and its principles followed, slavery has been abolished. It happened in ancient Rome, Britain, and the United States. Pray for the gospels spread and for the freedom of those still held in slavery.

Africans carry everything on their heads

CONTENT

*"I know what it is to be in need, and I know what it
is to have plenty. I have learned the secret of being
content in any and every situation, whether well fed
or hungry, whether living in plenty or in want."*

PHILIPPIANS 4:12

In mid-week, Emily informed Joan that they were invited for tea with the wife of United States Ambassador Matthews. Mrs. Matthews had tea once a week to welcome new Americans to Lagos. It was an unexpected pleasure for Joan. Only four days earlier she had been stranded under a tree, in the bush, next to a broken car. Now she was seated at an elegant tea party at the ambassador's residence. The ambassador's wife was pleasant, gracious, and made everyone feel welcome. On this beautiful tropical morning, tea was served on the patio in a beautifully landscaped yard. Joan said she felt a bit awed, but thoroughly enjoyed her morning tea.

When John learned that I enjoyed tennis, he made arrangements with the tennis professional at his private club. I was sure I was not ready for this, but why turn down a once in a lifetime opportunity. I felt rather privileged as I was chauffeured to my match. The young lady, who was the club professional, was very pleasant and friendly. She made playing delightful and passed on several tips to improve my game.

On our last night with the Langley's there was a cocktail party in our honor. I certainly had not expected this. John and Emily invited a large number of physicians from the capital city. Some guests were from the American Embassy, while others were expatriate physicians on various assignments with the Nigerian government. There was also a large contingent of Nigerian physicians from the large hospitals there. After months alone in the bush, I was delighted to have so many stimulating conversations with medical colleagues. Most were unfamiliar with "bush" medicine.

Finally, John had noticed my interest in several electronic catalogs from Japan. We talked on several occasions, and he knew how much we wanted a tape player. We had recorded hundreds of hours of gospel music, popular music, and Christian hymns prior to coming out to the field. We had not brought a tape player as we were told they were available here. Unfortunately, with the civil war, they were no longer available and the duty on imports was prohibitive. "Let me bring it in for you through the diplomatic pouch," John said. "That way it will be duty free. I will go down to the docks and forward it to your mission when it arrives."

"I know what it is to be in need, and I have learned to be content in any and every situation…" (Philippians 4:12) Perhaps more correctly I should say that I am learning to be content. True contentment can only come by maintaining a right relationship with God. True contentment can only come as we learn and allow Christ to live in and through us. Have you, or are you, learning contentment?

DARKNESS

"The light shines in the darkness,
but the darkness has not understood it."

JOHN 1:5

The Grey's are leaving on furlough this week. They will be leaving several days early because they will also have to drive to Jos. As I will have to spend a great deal more time at the hospital, even informal language study is very difficult.

I have, however, struck up a new acquaintance in town. He is an elderly Muslim man whose name is Ali Amadu. He is the local Muslim priest who calls the people to prayer or "salla' five times a day. He speaks some English and has agreed to meet with me to help with my conversational Hausa. He is agreeable to meet whenever I can find the time.

After our first meeting, he took me to his home on the outskirts of Takum. His compound was separated from the outside world by an eight foot fence made of woven grass. Inside the compound, were three small huts and many children. He proudly introduced me to his three wives and several of the children playing there.

At our weekly meetings we occasionally meet at his home but more often at his small tailor's stall in the village. He is an important man in the Muslim community and many stop by to greet him. This will allow me to develop many new acquaintances in the Muslim community.

Our discussions covered "abin duniya" or everything in the world. He especially enjoyed discussing religion and prided himself on his Bible knowledge. His concept of Christianity and Mohammedanism is that we both strive by good works to build-up merit in heaven. As far is he is concerned, we will both get to heaven, just on a different path. He does not see that our "good works" cannot earn us a place in heaven. He does not understand that "good works" are simply the fruit of our gratitude to God for what He has already done for us in Jesus Christ. There is no need for "Grace" in Mohammedanism. Our friendship and discussions should prove interesting in the months ahead. Hopefully, I can help him understand the truth.

"The light shines in the darkness, but the darkness has not understood it..." (John 1:5) My friend, Ali Amadu, did not see the light although he read the Bible. Today in the western world the majority of the people, especially its youth, are rejecting the light. Does your light still shine amidst the darkness and increasing paganism around you? Does your life reflect the light? Are you always ready to give an answer for the hope that is in you?

MOON LANDING

*"Give thanks to the LORD, for He is good, His love
endures forever. 5Who by his understanding made
the heavens, His love endures forever."*

PSALMS136:1, 5

I n the early morning hours the house was dark, almost black,
although a bright full tropical moon stood high in the sky. I
crawled out of my mosquito netting and tuned my radio to the
Voice of America. While I stood staring at the tropical moon,
the voice of Neil Armstrong crackled over my short wave radio.
"The eagle has landed." It was February 21, 1969.

It was several months later that my father sent me a large
collection of photographs. These photographs were taken
from several popular magazines, including *Life, Time,* and
National Geographic, and were a visual report of what I had
heard over the radio months before. I could hardly wait for
my weekly visit with Ali Amadu.

Although it was nearly noon, the moon was still visible
in the sky. I sat on the bench next to Ali eager to share this
enormous scientific achievement. I explained the moon
landing as best I could and shared the photographs with him.

He did not seem particularly impressed, and I am sure he did not understand what had been accomplished.

As with other African friends with whom I had shared the pictures, it was beyond their comprehension. They lived in the "bush" of Africa. Their only transportation was on foot or perhaps by bicycle. While familiar with cars and trucks, few had ever ridden in them. They saw the mission aircraft regularly, but even fewer had ever flown. All had little or no education; none had a telephone, television, or running water, and most had never even seen a paved street. Rocket ships and a moon landing were beyond their comprehension.

In the "bush" what was understood was only what could be seen, touched, or experienced. What was understood was the daily need for food, clean water, the frequent deaths of the very young, the never ending problems with disease, the threat poised by poisonous snakes, and the struggle for life and sustenance.

"Who by his understanding made the heavens, His love endures forever." (Psalm 136:5) It is not important whether my African friends understand about the moon landing. It is most important that they understand the Lord who made the heavens; the Lord whose love endures forever and extends even here to those in the "bush" of Africa. Do you understand? Do you pray daily for those who do not?

ISOLATION

"So do not fear, for I am with you;
do not be dismayed, for I am your God..."

ISAIAH 41:10

When we arrived here nearly a year ago, not enough rain had fallen during the rainy season. By the end of the dry season, our wells were nearly dry and we were rationing water both in our homes and at the hospital. This year the rainy season had been excessively heavy. There is still more than a month of the rainy season left, and we are already nine inches above the normal rainfall.

Increasingly, we are becoming more isolated. The Katsina Ala River is now well over a half-mile outside its banks. This isolates us from the road to Jos and from our larger mission station at Mkar. The river is now so flooded that the barge can no longer ferry cars or trucks across. The only crossing is by canoe and that was nearly a forty-five minute trip. Even the small stream running through the village of Takum is flooded, blocking our regular route to town.

The roads in many places are washed out because of the heavy rains. Last week Reverend Persenaire made the trip from

Mkar to Jos. He added nearly 100 miles to his trip because of the bad roads. Even with the detours, he was stuck in the mud over twenty times and nearly ran out of cash paying villagers to push his car free. We have been advised to not attempt any trips by road.

Mail delivery is now very irregular. Our aircraft remain grounded by government order and the roads are a mess. A few weeks ago the last vehicle to bring mail down to the bush lost a sack of mail. The back door of the station wagon came open and no one noticed it. No one noticed it until two suitcases also fell out. They retraced their trip for many miles, but the lost mail was never found. To hear everyone talking about it, the lost mail would probably now fill a ship.

I took the precaution of typing and crossing everyone's blood on this side of the river. We are now on our own. Whatever happens, we have to deal with all the emergencies here. I am particularly concerned about the five missionary mothers due to deliver in the next few months.

"So do not fear, for I am with you; do not be dismayed, for I am your God…" (Isaiah 41:10) There was a false sense of security when the aircraft were flying and the roads were open. That is all now gone. Ultimately, no matter what our options, we are secure only with God. Perhaps adversity is only God's reminder of where we should put our trust. What makes you feel secure?

Malam Simon assisting Harry on rounds

Mae Mast-Nursing Supervisor

MALARIA

"...Now Simon's mother-in-law was suffering from a high fever and they asked Jesus to help her. So he bent over and rebuked the fever, and it left her..."

LUKE 4:38-39

One of the most common diseases in West Africa is malaria. It is one of the leading causes of death in children in Africa and worldwide. Those who survive have multiple recurrences of the disease throughout their lifetime. As a practical matter, every individual who comes to the hospital with a fever is first treated for malaria. We then continued to search for other causes of their fevers.

The majority of Africans do not take preventive medications and few have mosquito netting. The availability and cost of these items is a major problem as well as their acceptance by the population. Education once again is crucial.

The majority of missionaries are faithful in taking their prophylactic medications and in using mosquito netting over their beds. Most children hated the medication because of its bitter taste. Even with these precautions, few leave the mission field without an attack of malaria. Every expatriate mother who gave birth on the field has an attack of malaria post delivery. It does not seem to matter what preventative medication they are taking.

Expatriates are also susceptible to a type of malaria known as "cerebral malaria." It is not as common among the native population. It occurs when the malaria invades the brain. It causes death in 15 to 20 percent of the cases. Those who survive may have lifelong neurological impairments as a result of the disease.

Malaria is not a pleasant experience. Along with the intermittent high fevers come marked fatigue, joint aches, and pains. The headaches are excruciating and are accompanied by shaking chills. If medication is given promptly, the acute fever passes in a day or so. However, it would still be several days before one began feeling normal once again.

"...Now Simon's mother-in-law was suffering from a high fever and they asked Jesus to help her. So he bent over and rebuked the fever, and it left her..." (Luke 4:38-39) Many believe that it was malaria affecting Peter's mother-in-law. Malaria continues its harvest of death and morbidity today in tropical countries. Pray for these individuals and support the efforts to supply mosquito netting and drugs to those who cannot afford them.

A MIST

*"...What is your life? You are a mist that appears
for a little while and then vanishes."*

JAMES 4:14B

Sunday was Joan's 27th birthday. It started out quietly enough, as she accepted our congratulations and opened a few small gifts at the breakfast table. This morning we were to have family worship at home. The children occasionally needed a break from the Hausa service we normally attended; that service is very long and the concrete benches very hard. It is even harder to sit quietly when only snatches of the language are understood.

Christy suddenly left her chair and lay down on the kitchen floor. "Daddy, I feel cold," she said. She then began to shiver violently. I picked her up and headed to her bedroom. Within a few minutes her temperature was over 105 degrees. I suspected malaria because of the rapid onset of symptoms and the lack of other findings. Joan began sponging her with wet towels while I raced to the hospital for an injectable form of anti-malarial medicine. I prayed silently as I raced on my motorcycle.

When I returned a few minutes later, Christy appeared very ill. Her lips were blue, she was delirious, and then after a brief seizure, she appeared to stop breathing. I turned her over and was about to start artificial resuscitation when she took a spontaneous breath. I quickly injected the Cloroquine phosphate for her malaria. Then once again I attacked the fever, sponging her with moist cool towels. I feared cerebral disease, the most severe form of Falciparum malaria.

This was a time when being the only doctor was most difficult. Caring for a loved one with a serious, possibly life threatening disease, and then trying to make cool, clinical, decisions without emotional interference. There would be no second opinion and no other consultation.

Fortunately, a few hours later Christy started improving. Her fever was resolving and she was able to speak and even sit up. Her seizure was most likely the result of her very high fever and not cerebral malaria. She fully recovered in two days.

What is your life? It is but a mist that appears for a little while and then vanishes? Joan said at that moment she realized that our children were not our own, but belonged to God. He can take them at anytime. They are ours, but only for a little while. Do you possess your children? Or have you given them back to God like Hannah. They are His you know. Let them go where He leads them.

ENOUGH

"But how can I bear your problems and your
burdens and your disputes all by myself?

DEUTERONOMY 1:12

Work at the hospital was continuing smoothly. I had adjusted to a routine of surgery and daily rounds. I was very busy, but so far the routine had allowed me to keep my head above water. The daily surgeries, both elective and emergent, however, still at times made me anxious.

The past two weeks have been nearly unbearable. In addition to the daily routine, there have been major surgical emergencies each night for the past ten nights. These patients arrived late at night carried on stretchers born on the heads of two bearers. Most of these patients had been carried for more than 20 miles.

Most of the emergency surgeries dealt with incarcerate or strangulated hernias. The past two weeks has also brought a ruptured ectopic pregnancy and an emergency C-section. There was also one gangrenous orthopedic emergency and two acute abdomens secondary to infection. One of the cases had multiple typhoid perforations.

During the past two weeks, it seemed, I would no sooner put my head on the pillow when I would hear the ringing of a small bicycle bell outside my window. Rising up on one arm I could look through the mosquito netting and out of my bedroom window. There in the grass, astride his bicycle, I would see one of my assistants, a kerosene lantern in his free hand. "Garfari Likita, Garfari" the soft-spoken voice would ask. In English, excuse me doctor excuse me, "We have a emergency at the hospital and need you right away."

In the pitch-like darkness, I would first shine a flashlight on the floor to check for unwanted visitors. Then I turned over my shoes to empty them of any scorpions. Dressing quickly, flashlight in hand, I walked to the back porch and pushed my motorcycle into the yard. It took only a few minutes after that to reach the hospital. Before entering, I would also start the generator so there would be light to examine the patient and possibly operate.

I was so tired at the end of the two weeks; I prayed that God would stop the constant flow of emergencies. Graciously, there were no more emergencies at night for nearly another week.

"...How can I bear your problems... all by myself?" (Deuteronomy 1:12) I confess sometimes I felt a little like Moses when his father-in-law told him he needed more help. Unfortunately, there were no more doctors. Busy, sometimes stressed, often tired, I was pushed to the limit of what I could handle. Then God answered my prayer and temporarily stopped the nightly flow of emergencies. To what or to whom do you go first with your stress and problems?

HONESTY

"Whoever can be trusted with very little can also
be trusted with much, and whoever is dishonest
with very little will be dishonest with much."

LUKE 16:10

Joan had an interesting situation handling the household help this past week. Two-and-a-half months ago our houseboy, Zachariah, told Joan he would like to go back to school. Joan encouraged him to take the tests and offered him a week to do so, but if he was returning to school, Joan wanted to know. She would then have to find other help in the house.

Zachariah took his week off and then returned to his job. He worked for another week and then disappeared without another word. No one in his village knew his whereabouts. We continued to inquire about him for several days through others who knew him. No one knew where he had gone or when he was returning. We did learn he had not returned to school.

Joan still needed help in the house with cleaning, laundry, preparing meals, and baking bread three times a week. So eventually she brought our yard boy, John, into the house and began training him to perform the household duties. He proved to be a very apt pupil and was soon performing the household tasks better than Zachariah had done. His bread, in fact, was nearly as good as the bread Joan had been baking.

Nearly two months went by before Zachariah reappeared wishing to go back to work. He expected to immediately have his old job back as if he had never been gone. He gave no explanation for his absence. He was upset for nearly a week at now having to work outside instead of inside the house. He did accept the job and worked for us until we left the country. We never learned the reason for his absence.

Dishonesty is a two edged sword. While initially it may get you what you desire, eventually others have difficulty trusting you. Giving your word is only good if you keep it. Then it has great value and you may be trusted with a great deal more. How good is your word? Is it trustworthy?

Zachariah carries 55 gallon drum home

JUDGE AND JURY

"Do not judge, or you too will be judged.
For in the same way you judge others,
you will be judged, and with the measure you use,
it will be measured to you."

MATTHEW 7:1-2

This morning a fifteen-year-old Kutev boy was brought to the hospital. He had been accused of stealing a bicycle nearly a week ago. A mob of villagers caught and beat him. They then tied his wrists tightly together. Three days later the police found the bicycle and determined the young boy was innocent. Searching for him, they found and rescued him from his accusers. His hands and wrists were still tightly bound.

When he arrived at the hospital six of his fingers, three on each hand, had bare bones protruding from rotting flesh. On his left hand, his thumb and middle finger, although discolored and infected, appeared viable. On his right, the thumb and index finger were similarly infected with bone protruding from the tip of the index finger.

Vigilante justice is not uncommon in Africa. Suspected criminals are immediately set upon by mobs without trial or jury. Many are horribly abused. Vigilante "justice" is frequently not just.

I admitted him to the hospital and began IV antibiotics along with frequently changed moist dressings. He needed a hand surgeon, but I would have to do. Thirty-six hours later, I took him to surgery and debrided the obviously necrotic tissue from six of his fingers. There was nothing but bare bones remaining and those six fingers were removed at the base. The tip of the index finger was also removed on the right hand.

I left the wounds open and continued IV antibiotics and moist dressing. Three days later I took him back to surgery to close all of the wounds.

He was released from the hospital ten days later. He still had two functioning fingers on each hand. Most importantly both of his thumbs had survived. Months later, as I passed through his village, he ran to me and greeted me with a warm hug and a broad smile. He then demonstrated the facility of his remaining fingers. I was delighted in how well he had done and that he would be able to earn a living and not be reduced to begging.

"Do not judge or you too will be judged... and with the measure you use, it will be measured to you." (Matthew 7:1-2) How easily we form judgments about those around us. How quickly we dispense justice in thought or deed. We do need to evaluate the individuals we associate with and the behaviors we imitate. But we must leave it to God to judge and dispense judgment. Are you a judge and jury?

SPIRITUAL RETREAT

*"Let us not giving up meeting together, as some are
in the habit of doing, but encouraging one another—
and all the more as you see the Day approaching."*

HEBREWS 10:25

One of the joys of missionary service was the annual spiritual retreat. This year the spiritual retreat was held at Mkar, by far our largest station. The retreat was always a large logistical problem for the hosts. In addition to the families stationed there, they must absorb well over two hundred other people. Most children accompany their parents and no one, missionary or child, wanted to miss it. It was a wonderful time of fellowship, renewing old acquaintances, and making new ones.

The most difficult problem was finding housing for everyone during the four-day conference. This year, after the mission houses and the guest houses were filled, the large overflow was assigned to the student housing at the teacher's college. The grass huts were a little inconvenient, offering only a sleeping mat on the dirt floor. There was no electricity, running water, or doors. Nearly all the children loved it, but the mothers were left to worry about the dirt and the real possibility of lice.

Joan and the children were able to attend the entire conference, while I was able to attend the last two days. One of the doctors from Mkar, Dr. Keith Platte, relieved me for the last two days. He had attended the first two days with his family.

Joan was delighted when I arrived. I have no doubt that tending the children in the hut was a chore. Another pair of hands was more than welcome. Some of the children in the other huts were afflicted with lice, while ours were thus far free of the nuisance. The guest speaker was excellent and Joan and I thoroughly enjoyed the afternoon and evening lectures.

Fellowship with our colleagues continued well into the night. There was no rain and those of us in the huts sat around a roaring fire, often until after midnight. We would "perk" repeated pots of coffee over the fire while enjoying the company, conversation, encouragement, and stimulation of our fellow Christians and workers.

"Let us not giving up meeting together, as some are in the habit of doing, but encouraging one another—and all the more as you see the Day approaching." Hebrews 10:25

What are your Sunday habits? Do you go to church only when you feel like it or do you feel it is too important to miss? It is your spiritual retreat every week. A time to encourage or to be encouraged. A time to speak and a time to listen. A time to reflect and a time to grow. Don't miss It!

REFRESHED

"For they refreshed my spirit and yours also.
Such men deserve recognition."

1 CORINTHIANS 16:18

The work at the hospital continued unabated. All of the beds are full, and we have a number of patients sleeping on the floor. Fortunately, Dr. Keith Platte has just arrived from Mkar and will be assisting me for the next two weeks. It was a most welcome relief. I have almost forgotten how it felt to have a second physician, someone else to take night calls or to make rounds. I was glad to have an added pair of hands for a difficult surgery and someone with whom I could discuss a difficult situation and get a second opinion.

Four of our local missionary wives are due for delivery within the next six weeks. I delivered a fifth mother one week ago. She had a healthy little boy. That week we learned of the death of a technician at Columbia University Hospital in New York City and the near death of one of the virologists. The virologist was involved in the research of the new African fever. The technician had no known contact with the disease. It previously killed two of the nurses at our sister mission in Jos. It appears to be viral, but its transmission was still unknown. Fortunately, we have not seen any cases of the deadly fever here in the bush. I am increasingly glad that I had decided to deliver the missionaries' wives here.

Normally, most of the missionary wives went to Jos where there was more help and facilities, but since our aircrafts are still grounded and the roads questionable, keeping everyone here seems wise. Keith, however, can only stay here for two weeks and I will be alone when Joan delivers. Doctors ordinarily avoided caring for their own family because of the strong emotional attachment they have with the patient. Approaching a patient in a purely clinical manner is more difficult with those one loves deeply. I had already experienced that with Christy's severe malarial attack and would soon find myself in a similar position with Joan.

Keith has already returned to Mkar. There was only one other physician there and they needed two more than I, as it was a larger hospital. Obviously, it was far from ideal for two large hospitals to have three physicians between them. The normal complement was six. None of the other missionary wives delivered while Keith was here so there were still four to go. I cannot express, however, how helpful it was to have him here the past two weeks. Not only sharing the workload, but mentally. Finally there was a break from the responsibility of making every decision and dealing with every surgery or disease problem. That was a great, even if only a temporary, relief.

"For they refreshed my spirit and yours also. Such men deserve recognition." (1 Corinthians 16:18) Have you ever been in a situation where the problems and decisions never stop? Decisions that may mean life or death? Decisions you have to make? The Apostle Paul had three visitors who refreshed his spirit as Keith refreshed mine.

BLOOD

"He will rescue them from oppression and violence,
for precious is their blood in his sight."

PSALM 72:14

A second missionary mother delivered last night. It was another healthy baby boy. However, the delivery brought back all the fears and anxiety of delivering the women here alone in the "bush." It was a very long and difficult labor, complicated by a post-postpartum hemorrhage. Her uterus simply refused to contract after the delivery. Finally, after extensive uterine massage and two shots of Pitocin, the heavy bleeding slowed and then stopped. It was obvious from the patient's pallor, rapid heart rate, and low blood pressure that she had lost a considerable amount of blood. Her IV fluids would help maintain her blood volume, but she needed a transfusion. It was now 2:00 a.m. and the head nurse and I were alone.

The hospital did not have a blood bank as we had no way of freezing the blood for storage. I did not wish to try and find a donor from the high school, because of the high risk of malaria, hepatitis, and parasitic disease common among the native population. However, several months ago, I had typed and crossed all the missionaries and their dependents living on this side of the river. We would need one of them as soon as possible.

My head nurse, Mae Mast, ran to her office and found our missionary blood list. She quickly found a match for the patient in a male colleague living six miles away. She then ran and awakened a missionary living here at Takum. He dressed quickly and then raced away in the dark on his motorcycle to the home six miles away. There he pounded on the door and awakened the startled missionary. The missionary agreed to help immediately and hopped on the motorcycle for the ride back to Takum.

Once our donor arrived, I placed him on a table parallel to the patient, only four inches higher. A large #18 needle was placed into his arm while the #18 needle on the other end of the rubber tubing was placed into the patient's. This direct patient-to-patient transfusion I had only performed once in my medical career, and it happened that night in the bush of Africa. Fortunately, it was without complications. The donor had no problems and our patient had immediate improvement. The rest of her postpartum recovery was normal.

"He will rescue them... for precious is their blood in his sight." (Psalm 72:14) God knew, but I did not, how important typing and crossing of all the missionaries was to be. Thankfully, I never had to do a person-to-person transfusion again.

CHILDREN

"...And a little child will lead them."

ISAIAH 11:6

The rainy season continues. Last year we prayed for rain, and this year we pray for the rain to stop. It has far exceeded the needs of everyone including the African farmers. Even rice is rotting because of the rain.

The storm last night was a real doozy. Joan, who is near full term, decided to remain home Sunday night with Christy. Three-year-old Tim and I rode my Honda to the Combine School for the evening service with the students. As we left the house, Tim looked up at the sky and said, "It's going to rain Dad." I looked at the gathering clouds and thought so too, but felt it would hold off for a few hours.

We rode to the Combine School and midway through the evening service it suddenly became very dark. Thunder rolled and lightening flashed across the sky. Tim and I quickly left the service hoping to beat the now rapidly approaching storm. The clouds above us were dark, rolling, and frightening.

It now looked like night as we climbed on the motorcycle for the trip home. Less than a mile down the road the storm struck like a whirlwind. Amidst repeated peals of thunder and jagged streaks of lightening, the rain came down like it was poured from a bucket; a real torrential downpour. Riding into the driving rain only made the deluge seem heavier. We arrived home some twenty minutes later, at the height of the storm, resembling a pair of drowned rats. Not one stitch of our clothing was dry. From the mouths of children...

Inside the house, close lightening strikes sparked and sizzled from our wall sockets while the strong smell of ozone filled the house. The storm was as frightening inside as it was outside. We later learned that an African Evangelist and his guest were struck and killed inside a hut. Here, our homes are often the highest point as we lack the many tall trees common back home. The lightening seemed so close. We prayed for safety in the home even as Tim and I had prayed out in the storm.

"...And a little child shall lead them." (Isaiah 11:6) God gave parents the responsibility of training and teaching the children in the home. But do you ever listen to your children? You should and if you do, you will learn important truths about family relationships. Truths that may actually improve how you lead and teach. It will certainly improve your relationships with them.

FULANI BEATING

"Whoever spares the rod hates his son, but the one who loves him is careful to discipline him."

PROVERBS 13:24

Today I observed a traditional Fulani custom. While in town near the market, I saw a large circle of Fulani teenagers, both boys and girls. In the center of the circle two young men, about 15 years old, appeared to be fighting. I moved closer and over the heads of the teenagers I saw the two young men at the center of the crowd's attention.

They were both bare to the waist but were not fighting. One young man was whipping the other with a long flexible branch about 3/8 inch in diameter. The boy stood with his chest exposed and made no effort to avoid the blows; linear, raised, red wheals crisscrossed his chest and upper abdomen. Some of them were open and bleeding. His mouth was wet with saliva stained orange by the Kola nuts he was chewing for pain.

A circle of mostly young teenage girls stood around the young men. They were dressed in their finest and wore long dangling earrings. Their lips were reddened and their faces colored by traditional cosmetics. All wore broad smiles and chattered incessantly. As unlikely as it appeared, it was a festive occasion. Each strike of the whip was punctuated by the loud shouts and trills of the crowd. This ceremony is known as a Fulani beating.

Once a year young boys of the tribe are paired with a partner. On the first day one partner beats the other. The second day, the one beaten beats his partner. This I am sure serves to control the severity of the beatings. The object is for the young boys to show they are ready to take their place among the men of the tribe. They do this by taking the beating and not crying out. A living example of our English adage, "Take it like a man." Now I understand the scars on the chest of all Fulani men.

Once a young boy proves he is a man, he must take a bride, hence the predominance of attractive young girls at each ceremony. At first glance, this test of manhood seems cruel and primitive. Yet when one looks at our Modern Western societies, there is a dearth of defining traits that mark the passage from childhood into manhood or young womanhood. Many seek to prove their adult status by engaging in various risky behaviors including drugs, smoking, alcohol, sexual experimentation, and disrespect of authority. You decide who has it right.

"Whoever spares the rod hates their children, but the one who loves their children is careful to discipline them." (Proverbs 13:24) The Bible is not condoning beating your child. The term rod is a concrete example for all discipline. But he who does not discipline his children really does not love them. Do you discipline your children? The Bible says that discipline imparts wisdom and discourages foolish behavior. What attitudes or behaviors do you accept in your home? Discipline with love because you love and care.

MARKED

*"...Go throughout the city of Jerusalem and put a
mark on the foreheads of those who grieve and lament
over all the detestable things that are done in it."*

EZEKIEL 9:4

I n Africa, tribal identity seems to be paramount for each individual. It is to the tribe that most give their loyalty and allegiance. National unity and concern for other tribes is more difficult. The hundreds of different languages and customs are often insurmountable barriers.

The African continent has a vast number of different tribes. There are literally thousands of different ethnic groups each with its own language, customs, and tribal area. In Nigeria alone there are over two hundred fifty. Some groups are small while others may number in the millions. At the hospital we served twenty-five different tribal peoples. The longer one interacted with them, the easier it became to recognize the various tribes. There are distinct differences in dress, language, appearance, and in their tribal markings.

Nigerians, especially, use tribal markings to identify their tribes. I have been told that an expert in tribal markings could identify an individual to tribe, clan, and family by simply looking at his or her face. Tribal markings are put on at an early age. Thus children have nothing to say. In my experience most marks were on the face or chest and were more elaborate in females than in males.

Some Nigerian tribes prefer a type of marking using ink tattoos. Other tribes prefer a type of marking that was made permanent by scarification. These tribal markings are etched into the skin of the face and chest with a nail or other sharp object. This is done between the ages of five and eight years of age. Then ashes from the fire are rubbed into the etching to encourage a thicker more prominent scar. It seems mutilating but I often found many attractive. They also gave each individual a clear sense of identity and the assurance of belonging. We again may quickly judge this behavior as primitive. Yet in our own culture youth, and some adults, seek identity by mutilating their own bodies with tattoos and multiple body piercings.

"...Go throughout the city of Jerusalem and put a mark on the foreheads of those who grieve and lament over all the detestable things that are done in it." (Ezekiel 9:4) Ezekiel speaks of marking those faithful to God and Revelation speaks of those bearing the mark of the beast. The Apostle Paul said he bore the marks of Christ through his suffering for Him. Have you been marked? Does your life and behavior identify you as belonging to the family of God?

ANXIETY

"Do not be anxious about anything, but in everything, by prayer and petition, with thanksgiving, present your requests to God. And the peace of God, which transcends all understanding, will guard your hearts and your minds in Christ Jesus."

PHILIPPIANS 4:6-7

It was 3:00 a.m. when Joan woke me from a deep sleep. "I have been having contractions for forty-five minutes and they are getting stronger," she said. I dressed quickly and lit the kerosene lantern, as Joan got out of bed to find her clothing. I then ran across the dark compound, flashlight in hand, to the home of Ruth VanderMolen. I pounded on the door to awaken her. Through the door she assured me she would soon be at our home to care for the other children. I then ran to the far end of the compound to awaken Mae Mast for her assistance in the delivery room. Finally, I ran back home to take Joan to the hospital.

At home I found Joan making her way to the front door, pausing with each new contraction. Ruth arrived at nearly the same time, and the two of us helped Joan into the small truck parked near our front door. We drove quickly to the hospital, and there we found Mae waiting for us with a lantern in her hand.

We quickly positioned Joan on one of the surgical tables, and Mae began prepping and covering her with sterile drapes. I turned to run back outside to start the generator. "Don't leave, the baby is coming," Joan exclaimed. With her history of rapid deliveries, I did not need to be told a second time. I had just enough time to put on a pair of sterile gloves and make a small episiotomy. As Mae held the lantern high, the infant's head appeared and our third child, Debra Lynn, was quickly delivered into the world. A very dimly lit world, full of giant shadows cast on the wall by the light of the kerosene lantern.

I offered a silent prayer of thanks for the quick, normal delivery and the lack of abnormal bleeding. "Yes Lord, I was anxious," I confessed. After delivering the placenta, I went back outside and started the generator. I then returned and repaired the small episiotomy. Soon mother and child were back in the truck and I put them both to bed with Ruth's help. She promised to return in the morning to give both of them a bath.

"Do not be anxious about anything, but in every situation, by prayer and petition, with thanksgiving, present your requests to God. [7] And the peace of God... will guard your hearts..." (Philippians 4:6-7) I was anxious and yet time after time God has been faithful. Are you ever anxious? Do the problems of this world make you doubt God? Pray that God may increase your faith. I do.

MAMBA

"Whoever digs a pit may fall into it; whoever breaks through a wall may be bitten by a snake."

ECCLESIASTES 10:8

We are fortunate to have some trees growing on our housing compound. Not only for the shade they provide, but also many are fruit trees. They were planted by other missionaries years ago. We never tire of the fresh fruit — lemon, papaya, grapefruit, and oranges. We have a rough lemon tree and a grapefruit tree near our house in the backyard. The children love to play around and in them.

Last week, I saw a ripe grapefruit hanging from the tree and went to pick it. My eyes were focused on a large one, which looked especially ripe. My hand was closing around the bottom of the fruit when I saw it. Six inches away, on an adjacent branch, a long green snake was stretched out, draped from branch to branch. The green color of the snake blended nearly perfectly with the green leaves of the tree. It appeared to be at least six feet long. Its head a few inches away never moved, but its beady eyes were fixed on me. I quickly stepped back pulling my hand away from the tree.

My heart was pounding as I turned and raced to the house to get a shovel. I silently thanked God for sparing my life and that the children had not been the ones to find it.

All Mambas are venomous. All are deadly, with venom that is primarily neurotoxic. Neurotoxic means the effect of the venom is primarily on the nervous system. The Africans know how deadly they are and call it the "two step snake." Basically, those who are bitten do not live long. Those who make a living harvesting the various fruit and nuts of palm trees are most likely to be bitten. It is a tree snake and usually lays high in the trees where it lives off of the birds it catches. Among those seen with snakebites at the hospital, it is probably the least common bite, but it is among the most deadly.

I quickly returned to the tree with shovel in hand. The snake was nowhere to be seen. Unlike its black cousin, the Green Mamba, is not nearly as aggressive but equally venomous. Needless to say, the children heard instructions about climbing in the trees without first looking at what else was in them.

"…Whoever breaks through a hedge may be bitten by a snake." (Ecclesiastes 10:8) I am glad it was not Joan picking the fruit. The children might never have gotten out of the house again. There are many types of poisonous snakes here in West Africa. Does your church send missionaries? Are you aware of the dangers they face? Do you pray daily for their safety?

JUKUN GOD

"You shall have no other gods before me."

DEUTERONOMY 5:7

What is left of the Jukun Empire in Nigeria is now centered in the town of Wukari, a town about fifty miles from Takum and a bit larger. Historically, the Jukun people go back hundreds of years and once ruled large areas of what is now Nigeria.

Rev. Ed Smith, a former long-term missionary here, gave some credence to the theory that the Jukun people may once have migrated from Egypt. This was based on several of the customs that the Jukun practiced which were native to Egypt. For instance, when the men reach a certain age, some wear a double string of braided hair at the back of their head. Secondly, they were naked from the waist up when in the presence of their king. Finally, their king was also considered divine as were the Pharaoh's of Egypt. None of this was, however, proven.

According to their traditions, the Jukun selected a new king every seven years. This was done by a select group of tribal elders called the Kingmakers. Their deliberations were made in secret, as was the crowning of the new king. Peculiar to the Jukun traditions, was the tradition of removing the old god by strangulation every seven years. This made way for a new ruler. He then moved into the palace and inherited the old god and king's wives and possessions.

Although this tradition was strongly believed, Reverend Smith said that he doubted its truth. During his nearly forty years in Nigeria, he had known at least four of the kings who ruled for more than ten years. Perhaps, he admitted, it was true in the past.

The present Jukun King had now ruled for nine years and was about to be the most famous patient at Takum Christian hospital.

The first commandment allows no other gods. We are to only worship the Creator God and Father of our Lord Jesus Christ. The Bible, however, does not say there are not other gods. Even today, some worship demons and the majority of people worship what the ancient idols represented; sex, fertility, prosperity, sports, or even mother nature. Do you have any other gods? Do you worship something created or the Creator?

LOSING ONE'S HEAD

*"'Skin for skin!' Satan replied. 'A man will give
all he has for his own life.'"*

JOB 2:4

An article in the international edition of *Newsweek* magazine, on December 29,1969, featured a full-page article about the Jukun King. The article was entitled, "Keeping One's Head," and alerted the world to his plight. The article said:

"To become the Aku Uka, the title born by the King of the Jukuns, a small pagan tribe in central Nigeria, is truly an elevating experience. Chosen from among the several royal houses, the Aku Uka is bathed in holy water and wrapped in a splendid robe crafted from the skins of rabbit, antelope, and jumping bush rat. Regally mounted on a white horse, the new King is then led away to his predecessor's palace. There he takes possession of the old King's household, dressed in his finery, drinking his beer, and making love to his bereaved widow. The world is yours, chants the high priest. May you come to the end of your reign in health."

"There is a catch, for tradition also decrees that the Aku Uka's reign is to last only seven years and that at the end of that period, the high priest and a group of elders must return to the palace in the dead of night and strangle the King in his sleep. That custom has been followed without a hitch for centuries. But two years ago, when his time came to be throttled, the present Aku Uka a former science teacher named Malam Adi Bdwaye, declined to go quietly. For months now he has been lurking in a shabby palace, sleeping fitfully with a loaded revolver at his side."

"The plight of the Aku Uka has set off a stormy debate in Nigeria, pitting the scandalized traditionalists against the young progressives. The latter agree with the fifty-five year old Aku Uka that his ritual demise would amount to premeditated murder. It is shameful that there should be a tribe in Nigeria still interested in human sacrifice said another young Nigerian."

Another article appeared in Nigeria's largest newspaper, *The Lagos Times*. The article was entitled, "Should this man surrender his head?" Of the 500 letters received, 225 letters voted against the Aku Uka. Nearly all sited respect for the ancient tribal traditions.

"...A man will give all he has for his own life." (Job 2:4) The Bible in the Gospel of John states that giving up one's life for another was the greatest form of love. Jesus not only spoke of loving us, He freely gave up His life to save each of us. Have you picked up your cross? Would you give up your life for Him as Christian martyrs continue to do today?

THE PATIENT

"You will be secure, because there is hope; you will look about you and take your rest in safety."

JOB 11:18

I had seen the Aku Uka several times at the hospital. It was always for minor problems, including a urinary tract infection. As the year 1969 came to a close, the Aku Uka was in Jos, the capital of our state. While there he was attending various meetings with other tribal leaders and the federal government.

To my surprise, I received a radio message on New Year's Day stating that the Aku Uka would be flown to Takum Hospital. He had become ill in Jos during the past week, and trusting few, had refused hospitalization there. He insisted on being flown to the Mission Hospital at Takum.

As I was completing my morning rounds, a Sudan Interior Mission plane flew low over the hospital, announcing the arrival of our patient. It was the first flight I had seen since the federal government grounded all small planes. The Aku was met at the airstrip and quickly brought to the hospital.

The immediate cause of his illness was apparent. The Aku Uka was comatose with heavy sonorous breathing. There was no movement of his right side in response to painful stimuli. His blood pressure was elevated, as was his blood sugar which was 300. He was overweight and appeared much older than his fifty-five years. He obviously had some sort of cerebral vascular accident.

Over the following two weeks, he made a remarkable recovery. He became fully conscious and his speech was only mildly affected. Although weak on the right side, he was able to walk and had full use of his right arm. His blood pressure was now only mildly elevated and his blood sugars were normal. Two Jukun guards stood twenty-four hour watch over his private room. One stood at attention with an old double barrel British shotgun while the second stood holding a seven-foot pole, topped with a fan of brown feathers. It looked like an old Hollywood movie set.

The Aku Uka was anxious for discharge and to return to his palace at Wukari. He was sent home with medication for his blood pressure and his diabetes. He was also given dietary instructions. He was told to return in one week or sooner if he had a recurrence of symptoms. In light of his obesity, diabetes, and high blood pressure, he was at a very high risk for a recurrence and was so informed. I hoped he would return for followup, but felt less sure he would continue his medications or watch his diet.

"You will be secure because there is hope; you will look about you and take your rest in safety." (Job 11:18) Even god-kings worry and pick their friends carefully. Are you secure? In what is your hope? In 1 Timothy 4:10, the Bible says to "...put our hope in the living God, the Savior of all men." Have you?

DEATH

*"All men are like grass, and all their glory is like the
flowers of the field; the grass withers and the flowers
fall, [25]but the word of the Lord stands forever..."*

1 PETER 1:24-25

Four days later, on January 17, 1970, the Aku Uka returned
to the hospital. I was told that the night before, he had
difficulty speaking and complained of generalized weakness.
Those symptoms cleared by morning. Unfortunately, more
severe symptoms recurred around noon that day. Within
minutes he was deeply comatose. Upon his arrival, his blood
pressure and blood sugars were normal. His clothing was
stained with urine and all of his extremities were flaccid. He
was deeply comatose and unresponsive to painful stimuli. He
was given IVs with medication and monitored throughout the
night. He died early the next morning on January 19, 1970.

In light of the recent world-wide publicity, I expected
the government to request an autopsy at the medical school
in Ibadan. I was unaware that an autopsy had never before
been permitted on an Aku Uka. In fact no mention of their
death was ever made for they were divine kings. I contacted

Commissioner David Ashu by radio and explained the cause of death appeared to be a severe cerebral hemorrhage. He in turn consulted with the military government.

Subsequently, I was given verbal approval to release the Aku Uka body to the Jukun people. The Ministry of Health asked me to sign the death certificate. The only request was that I be very explicit in writing the cause of death. They feared rumors once the Aku Uka's death was known. Later that day, his body was transferred back to Wukari in one of our mission cars. The body was accompanied by my letter to the district officer in Wukari. It explained that the body had been released based on the verbal approval of the military government. The government papers would arrive on the following day.

"All men are like grass, and all their glory is like the flowers of the field; the grass withers and the flowers fall, [25]but the word of the Lord is forever..." (1 Peter 1:24-25) One day all of us will die. When we are young we often act and feel that we are immortal. But many die at a very young age. Many who are old and frail are eager to die and pray for God to take them. Are you ready to die? Are you ready to meet God? If you believe in His word and in His Son there is nothing to fear. You will live eternally!

INCURABLE

*"...Go back and report to John what you have seen
and heard: The blind receive sight, the lame walk,
those who have leprosy are cleansed,
the deaf hear, the dead are raised, and the good
news is proclaimed to the poor."*

LUKE 7:22

Neonates died daily at the hospital from tetanus. Less common were the cases and deaths among the adults who contracted the disease. Among those who survived infancy, the incidence of tetanus was thankfully decreasing. For over fifteen years, the nurses have been actively immunizing the people both at the hospital and in their villages. Tetanus is a terrible disease with a death rate that approaches 60-80 percent yet today. It results in continuous spasms of the muscles of the body; spasms that can be so strong that they can break bones and dislocate joints. When the muscles involved with breathing are involved, most die, unless placed on ventilators. There were no ventilators in the bush of Africa.

I remember fondly an old grey haired gentleman who survived the disease. Initially, following recovery, his muscles were nearly rigid from the continuous spasms. He could barely move and was unable to stand without help. He slowly recovered and then on discharge posed proudly for a picture with me. Incredibly, he wore a Kansas State track and field sweatshirt, undoubtedly retrieved from some unknown expatriate's used clothing pile. He was very proud of the sweatshirt, while I was proud he had survived the disease.

Not as fortunate was a young Jukun mother, who arrived at our out-patient clinic yesterday. Seeing her, I immediately walked over to her wheelchair. Friends who were accompanying her said she had given birth four weeks earlier. Several days ago she became ill and was getting progressively worse.

The symptoms of the disease were obvious. Spasms of her masseter (jaw) muscles clenched her teeth together in what is commonly known as "lock jaw". The sustained contractions of other facial muscles resulted in a facial grimace. Contractions of her back muscles arched her neck and back posteriorly. Other muscular contractions caused milk to stream continuously from her lactating breasts. We immediately began aggressive treatment with IVs, antitoxin, penicillin, and sedation. She was severely ill and I had little hope. She died several hours later during the night.

Daily we are faced with medical and surgical problems beyond our abilities to heal. John's disciples were given the good news of the Kingdom of God. In His Kingdom, the Word was spoken and all were healed. How often in the "bush" I saw those for whom we could do so little. Patients I wished I could touch or speak the Word and heal. One day there will be no more death or disease. Pray for it.

CHRISTMAS LETTER 1969

"But the angel said to them, 'Do not be afraid.
I bring you good news of great joy that
will be for all the people.'"

LUKE 2:10

At times it is hard for us to realize that Christmas is here. There are no gaily decorated stores, no Christmas music, and no crowds of happy shoppers. Instead the sun is progressively hotter as the dry season continues. The air is filled with dust and smoke from burning grasses and trees. The scent of burning grass and wood is everywhere, and the night is lit by hundreds of bush fires. Natives everywhere are burning off the dying grasses to prepare their fields for the next growing season. Yet Christmas is nearly here and as we look back on the year of 1969, our hearts are full at the evidence of God's hand upon us and our many blessings.

Nearly two months ago our second daughter, Debra, was born. It was entirely a family production as her father did the honors at her birth. Christy and Tim are very happy with the new addition and have already set aside some of their favorite toys for her.

Both Christy and Tim have grown considerably. Christy has mastered the art of riding a two-wheeler and is reading simple introductory books. She is at times bored and is looking forward to being a "Hill Crestor" when she will begin boarding school in August. Tim has also matured since our arrival sixteen months ago. Once a shy boy who stayed close to home, he now roams freely around the compound. He often returns home with various creatures and other things that attract boys and distress their mothers.

Joan and I remained in good health for which we are grateful. The hospital occupies nearly all of my time. I am eagerly looking forward to my colleagues return at the end of next month. Joan remains very busy with our home and the family. Our latest addition, like all babies, has a way of demanding nearly all of her mother's time.

The work at the hospital continues to increase with an ever rising number of patients. Many have come and found relief from their illnesses, and many have found a Savior who can cleanse their souls. We have been severely short staffed nearly the entire year, but He has provided the strength. We have at times felt a bit depressed and He has provided His Spirit. We have at times fallen short in our weakness and He has given us His Grace. A wonderful Savior is Jesus My Lord!

"...'Do not be afraid. I bring you good news of great joy that will be for all the people.'" (Luke 2:10) Are you filled with great joy? Remember what God has done for you. Count your daily blessings and name them one by one. You will be filled with joy!

PEACE

"There is a time for everything, and a season for every activity under the heavens: ...a time to love and a time to hate, a time for war and a time for peace."

ECCLESIASTES 3:1, 8

The civil war in Nigeria is at long last over! In the eastern region, the Igbo forces have been defeated and surrendered to the government. I have no doubt that those of you outside of Africa learned about the peace before we did. There were no media broadcasts in the bush just a message relayed through the missionary bush radio network. We praised God for the end of the fighting and pray that General Gowon would make this a just peace.

General Gowon, as a boy, attended mission schools and is a Christian. His life indicates that his Christianity is real. He also idolized the American President, Abraham Lincoln. Like Lincoln, he expressed the desire that the nation accept their former enemies back as brothers and sisters. He celebrated the peace by calling the nation to two days of prayer.

For the Nigerian people, the peace allowed those displaced by the war to return to their homes. Farmers will be able to plant their crops once again. During the war, we saw far too many with malnutrition and nearer the fighting the malnutrition was much more severe. The price of food rose dramatically everywhere and there was often shortages of the staples. For the poor, competition for food was often devastating. It will take many months for the new crops to alleviate the suffering and for food to be plentiful once again.

We have heard stories that the Igbo's, who once lived in the north, were now returning to their homes and were being received peacefully. Some had buried their possessions before fleeing and incredibly this was said to include even large trucks. After removing them from the earth, they are returning to their former businesses and resuming their lives. Amazingly, former enemies, in many cases, were now at peace with one another.

Regrettably, there were also reports of former soldiers forming armed gangs; some engaged in robbing civilians, hijacking lorries, and there are reports of killings. It is rumored that a regiment of soldiers will be placed near Takum, as the army spreads its soldiers around the country, rather than disband them.

"…A time to love and a time to hate, a time for war and a time for peace." (Ecclesiastes 3:8) There always seems to be time for hate, wars, and rumors of wars. Do you pray for peace? Do you pray for the Kingdom where they no longer train for war but love one another?

VIPER

*"Paul gathered a pile of brushwood and,
as he put it on the fire, a viper, driven out by
the heat, fastened itself on his hand."*

ACTS 28:3

We continue to see two to three snakebite victims each week with an average of two deaths each month. By a wide margin, the bite of the carpet viper far exceeds those of the cobra, mamba, puff adder, or the Gaboon viper. The Gaboon viper is the largest of the poisonous snakes and injects the most venom. Its fangs are nearly 2-1/2 inches in length. Because of the deep injection of its venom, amputation of the bitten extremity is recommended for survival.

The carpet viper is the smallest of the poisonous snakes. It is, however, numerous and has adapted well to living around villages and people. Because of its small size, about thirty inches, most of its bites are on the foot. I often wondered how many bites could be prevented if the people had shoes or flashlights as they walked the paths at night.

In a United States Navy study, reported while I was in the military during the Vietnam War, we were given the following statistical information: In a poisonous snake bite only 50 percent of the time is venom injected. When venom is injected, only 25 percent of the time is the dose lethal. This probably explains why the witch doctor is successful in treatment with the majority of his patients. Unfortunately, statistics do not reveal to us which individual bites will be deadly.

One snakebite victim stands out in my mind. He awoke in his dark hut and felt something crawling over him. Suddenly, he felt a sharp pain in one of his arms. Reflexively, he reached out to catch what he felt was a large snake and was bitten as well on the other arm. When he arrived at the hospital, fang marks were apparent on both of his forearms. Both arms were grossly swollen to the shoulders. Blood and serum leaked from the wounds while blisters appeared over both arms. Immediately IV antitoxin was begun and continued over the next 48 hours.

The snakebite victim slowly improved, but developed gangrene in the skin over large portions of both arms, eventually nearly 60 percent of the skin sloughed from wrists to shoulders. Over the following weeks I performed a number of split thickness skin grafts. Eventually both arms healed with a mixture of scar tissue and new skin. Most importantly, both arms were still functional.

"...A viper, driven out by the heat, fastened itself on his hand." (Acts 28:3) Unlike the Apostle Paul, my African friend suffered a severe injury from the viper's bite. God did, however, spare his life. Our lives are really not our own and they can be taken from us in an instant. One is spared and another is taken. Are you ready to meet God?

BLIND GUIDES

"Leave them; they are blind guides. If a blind man leads a blind man, both will fall into a pit."

MATTHEW 15:14

My family and I attended the evening worship service. As the service neared its conclusion, a hospital staff member appeared outside a window near me. He quietly rang his bicycle bell. I slipped out of the service and was told about a new patient at the hospital. They felt he had a strangulated hernia. I told him to make preparations, and I would be there after the service. My wife drove the car and dropped me off at the hospital and then went home with the children.

After examining the patient, I took him to surgery. The surgery went well and although the hernia was incarcerated, it had not yet strangulated. After finishing the operation, my assistant suggested I go home. They would happily attend to the patient and then turn off the generator. As it was nearly 9:00 p.m. and I had not yet eaten, home sounded like a very good idea. As I left the hospital it dawned on me that I didn't have a flashlight. It was very dark and also had begun to rain.

A light on the hospital roof faintly illuminated the gravel path that led toward my home. Foolishly, I began the three-quarter mile walk. I proceeded briskly down the path for about 300 feet. Suddenly, the lights went out. I had not anticipated them turning the generator off so quickly. It was pitch black, and it was now raining heavily. The sky was covered with dark clouds so there was neither moon nor starlight. I remembered being near the first house before the lights went out. Now I could not see its shape or distinguish the roof from the sky. There were no other lights in the homes, and I felt as if I were standing in a cave. On one side of the path was a deep five-foot ditch. In the darkness, I could hear water running along its bottom. I would have to walk carefully parallel to it.

Slowly, I felt my way along the gravel path. Suddenly, I pitched headfirst down into the ditch. My glasses flew off, and the Bible I was carrying slipped from my hand. I landed in the water and grass at the bottom. In the darkness, I was unable to see my hand in front of my face. Slowly, I ran my hand along the grass trying to locate my glasses and the Bible. By now, both of my legs and my right arm burned with what felt like long scratches. As I searched blindly along the sides and bottom of the ditch, I thought about snakes. How often our African patients were bitten at night on these dark paths. I prayed silently, "Please God, no snakes down here." A few moments later I located my glasses and the Bible. On all fours I crawled up out of the ditch. With my bare feet I found the gravel path and slowly made my way home.

Jesus warned the people to not follow the direction and teaching of the Pharisees. "Leave them; they are blind guides…" (Matthew 15:14) Do you follow blindly? Who do you follow? Who or what gives you direction in life's decisions? In who or what do you trust?

REST

*"There remains, then, a Sabbath-rest for the
people of God; for anyone who enters God's rest also
rests from their works, just as God did from his."*

HEBREWS 4:9-10

Dr. Grey and his family arrived back in Takum the last
week of January. After nearly six months of working
alone, I was ready for a vacation. With two other families,
we traveled to a government run cattle ranch, high atop the
Obadu plateau. We managed to get the Kiekover, Korhorn, and
Holwerda families into two of the mission's station wagons.

The trip was nearly two-hundred miles and we arrived
at the base of the plateau in mid- afternoon. Glancing up,
our eyes traced the narrow winding gravel road as it wound
its way up the escarpment. As the cars climbed the plateau,
there were numerous hairpin turns and no safety fences. The
views were magnificent. The trip up was uneventful except
for the overheating of one of the vehicles. This forced us to
stop twice on the road, and the radiator consumed all that
remained of our drinking water.

It was worth the trip! Each family had a chalet, and tea
was served twice a day. Each morning we were awakened by

a knock on the door. While we enjoyed the tea, the waiter started a fire in our fireplace to take away the morning chill. This tradition of our English cousins, we all immediately adopted as our own. Christy and Tim were especially fond of it and were out of bed at the first knock on the door.

Meals were served three times a day in a common dining room. Nearly all of the food was grown on the ranch, including fresh beef and pork. There were many fresh vegetables and fruits, including, to our surprise, strawberries. The variety of food made the meals feel like a feast compared to our resources in the bush. After a year-and-a-half on powdered milk, the children were not ready for the fresh milk from the ranch's dairy cows. Joan and I loved it, but the children would not drink it unless diluted with water.

Days were full of fun. We played tennis each day with our friends, explored the ranch's grounds, and swam several times in a mountain pool beneath a small waterfall. We had forgotten how cold water could be, and the first dive into the pool took my breath away. The children also enjoyed the horses. It took a few days before they were ready to ride, but then we had a pleasant ride to the forested area at the back of the property. We hoped to see gorillas, but did not. The horses were also the reason our sugar bowl was always empty of sugar cubes when it left the chalet each morning. Christy and Tim were secretly filling their pockets to later share them with their equine friends.

"...For anyone who enters God's rest also rests from their works..." (Hebrews 4:10) Each week God has provided a day of physical rest from our work. Also, believers no longer work to earn their salvation, but rest in the finished work of Christ. Do you enjoying a Sabbath rest?

GUARDIAN

"He will not let your foot slip—he who watches over you will not slumber; indeed, he who watches over Israel will neither slumber nor sleep.

PSALMS 121:3-4

Before returning to Takum, our family took an extra four days to visit the Yankari game preserve about 150 miles from Jos. We were assigned to a traditional mud hut. The outside walls had been white-washed, and each hut had the traditional grass thatched roof. Modern improvements included cold running water, a flush toilet, and a single bare electric bulb for lighting.

The animals here were amazing. Large herds of antelope raced beside us while warthogs wallowed in the mud. There were monkeys, baboons, bush cows, elephants, and lions. Above us flew flamboyantly colored birds. The preserve was a fascinating zoo without bars or cages.

Our last day was most exciting. In late afternoon, we came upon a large herd of elephants of all ages. The safari truck stopped in a heavily wooded area, and our guide waved his arms cautioning all of us to be very quiet. In front of us, in the clearing, the elephants stood. Some pulled the foliage off the trees, others sprayed their bodies with dust to rid themselves of insects, and several infants clung tightly to their mothers' tail. One huge bull elephant stood watch over the herd. His large ears moved at right angles to gather every sound of possible danger. His ivory tusks were large and long. He stood beside a palm tree whose leaves partially obscured his head.

Fascinated by the herd, we nearly missed the reason for the guide's signal for silence. Another large elephant was making her way through the foliage near the truck. Her large padded feet muffled the sound. Her movement was barely audible. Her progress followed by the branches and foliage she displaced. Standing on the flatbed of the truck, we barely glimpsed her as she passed six feet away. We could see that the top of her back was several feet higher than the wooden racks of our now uncomfortably small truck.

Suddenly, a loud trumpeting drew our attention back to the herd. While the huge bull continued to trumpet loudly, his ears flared and his body swayed in agitation. Amidst the trumpeted responses of other elephants, the entire herd stampeded at right angles to us. The ground shook as the herd pounded the earth in its flight from us. It was a sight none of us will ever forget.

The bull elephant watched carefully over the herd. He was alert for any signs of danger. The Bible says "...he who watches over Israel will neither slumber nor sleep." (Psalm 121:4) What assurance! The Creator of heaven and earth watches over our lives. He neither slumbers nor sleeps. You may trust Him completely.

TRIALS

"Consider it pure joy, my brothers and sisters,
whenever you face trials of many kinds,
because you know that the testing of your faith
produces perseverance."

JAMES 1:2-3

We all returned to Takum well rested after our vacation. I was, however, unprepared for an unexpected request. During the Saturday evening volleyball game, Dr. Grey called me aside. He informed me that he and his wife were leaving for four months once again to go to the eastern region, but this time he would be organizing medical clinics with a rural health group instead of attending patients. He had received approval for this work from the executive committee.

After a year alone, I was amazed that I had not been given a warning about this possibility nor was my input solicited. It was not a part of our mission's responsibility, and, once again, Dr. Grey was to be loaned to them. Now he wished my blessing. Initially, I was shocked and reluctant. After a night of rest and prayer, I agreed. I had worked alone the past year and felt assured that I could do another four months. The Grey's left the following week.

Christy and Tim picked up some form of dysentery during our previous vacation. Christy had now recovered, but Tim continued with fever and diarrhea. He now has lost nearly 15 percent of his body weight. He appeared weak and thin and was very tired. I missed my colleague already. However, with IV fluids and oral hydration Tim slowly recovered and was once again his old self. This was a great relief to his parents.

Yesterday, during hospital rounds, an old taxi raced up to the hospital. In it was a young mother in her mid twenties. She was pregnant with her third child. While in the market, she had the onset of labor and thirty minutes later began gushing large quantities of blood. She was carried immediately to surgery with a probable diagnosis of placenta previa. She was soaked with blood, her heart was racing, her blood pressure was undetectable, and there were no fetal heart tones. An emergency Caesarian section was done under local anesthetic. With IV fluids and donated blood, the mother survived. The fetus was limp and did not respond to resuscitation. Unfortunately, that little life was unable to tolerate his mother's massive blood loss.

"Consider it pure joy, my brothers and sisters, whenever you face trials of many kinds..." (James 1:2) The Apostle James challenged us to look at trials in a different way. Rather than thinking of trials as a sign of God's displeasure, we are to look at them as God's instruments; instruments that will build our faith and give us perseverance. Trials frighten us and no one wants them, yet they are building blocks of our faith. Rest assured, God promises to never give us more than we can bear. Is your faith strong enough to bear trials?

GUINEA WORMS

*"...If you listen carefully to the voice of the
LORD your God and do what is right in his eyes,
if you pay attention to his commands and
keep all his decrees, I will not bring on you any
of the diseases I brought on the Egyptians,
for I am the LORD who heals you."*

EXODUS 15:26

There were many debilitating diseases in Nigeria. One of the worst was caused by the tiny larva of the guinea worm. It is an ancient parasite that was noted in Egyptian medicine about 1500 B.C. The disease is transmitted through drinking water from a pool or well infected by a tiny water flea. Initially, the parasite is a tiny thread-like worm. Tiny as it is at the beginning, the worm can grow to an incredible three feet inside the human body.

After ingestion, the parasite penetrates the bowel wall and begins its migration. Eventually, most will migrate to the skin of the lower extremity or foot. There a blister appears along with intense burning and itching. Patients attempting to ease the burning will often bathe the extremity in cool water. If the blister breaks, the worm releases hundreds of tiny larva to repeat the cycle in anyone else drinking water from the pool or stream where the extremity was bathed.

The only treatment available was an ancient one. Once the blister broke and the worm was visible, the patient tied it to a small stick. Daily the patients twist the small stick extracting the worm a few millimeters at a time. If fortunate, the patient will extract the entire worm in about three weeks. More often, these worms die within the body or break off as an extraction is attempted. Commonly, our x-rays of the pelvis and lower extremities show their large circular, calcified remains.

For the past two weeks I have been treating a patient in one of our wards. He has two large guinea worms protruding from two separate sores on his lower right leg. Two small sticks of bamboo, to which the respective worms are tied, dangle from the wounds. During this stage of the disease, most patients are incapacitated by pain, fever, swelling, and intense burning. This patient also has a severe secondary infection, and death may result from these infections or internal complications.

If all had filtered or clean water, the disease could be prevented. Unfortunately, almost all water sources are contaminated. Lack of knowledge leads those with the parasite to bathe in common water supplies while seeking relief from the intense burning.

"…If you listen carefully to the voice of the LORD your God and do what is right in His eyes… I will not bring on you any of the diseases I brought on the Egyptians." (Exodus 15:26) We live in a broken world of sin of our own making. We are visited by all of the diseases in this broken world. Rather than complain about the disease you may have, look at others about you and thank God for all the things you do not have.

COLONEL

*"Do not boast about tomorrow, for you
do not know what a day may bring."*

PROVERBS 27:1

When the Nigerian Civil War ended, the military government decided to not disband the army, but rather to distribute the soldiers to bases around the country. It was hoped the soldiers could be put to good use on civilian projects rather than returning to their homes. One such base was near Takum, and suddenly there were many soldiers in the town and at the hospital clinics.

I was never afraid of the soldiers, but the casual manner in which they handled their weapons and grenades sometimes made me nervous. This was especially true in the outpatient clinic where most were seen for treatment. When asked to undress, they would casually drop the grenades or throw down their machine guns. It was as if they failed to understand the lethal nature of the weapons they carried. Perhaps this was true, as most were simply tribesman before being drafted into the army.

This afternoon a Nigerian colonel was brought to the hospital. He had been involved in a motor vehicle accident a few hours earlier. His jeep had rolled over, and he was in a great deal of pain. His left lower leg was crudely wrapped with a splint of flat boards and cloth. It dangled limply at his side, and he was unable to bear weight on it. It was swollen and discolored particularly over the distal two-thirds of the lower extremity. Severe pain was elicited with moderate pressure over the largest bone of his lower leg.

After a pain shot, he was taken to x-ray. The x-ray soon confirmed the suspected diagnosis of a fractured tibial bone. A long leg splint was applied and the leg elevated. He was told a full cast would be applied after the swelling went down. If the pain again became severe, he could have another shot for pain. The colonel was settled in a "private room" near the end of one of our hospital wards. He thanked me for my care. Little did I realize how much this man's presence in the hospital would benefit me tomorrow.

"Do not boast about tomorrow, for you do not know what a day may bring." (Proverbs 27:1) We plan, but God determines what future plans come to fruition. Many Christians wisely acknowledge this and add, "the Lord willing," to their plans for tomorrow. Not only do we not know what will happen tomorrow, often we may not fully understand the significance of what happened today.

General Gomwalk arrives to tour the hospital, Harry, Harold Padding and Chief of Takum

Harry with Divine God and King of the Jukuns, "Aku Uka" Malam Adi Bdwaye

ANGER

"Better a patient person than a warrior,
one with self-control than one who takes a city."

PROVERBS 16:32

There are often problems that arise in communities near military bases. One of those problems is the need of soldiers for sexual companionship. At the hospital, we had a large number of young African girls. Some simply helped in cleaning the hospital, while others were in training. Last night our nursing supervisor, Mae Mast, was making late rounds when she discovered three of the soldiers involved in sexual activity with members of our staff. She sent the girls away and locked the soldiers in the room. They simply kicked the door down and returned to base.

The next morning, after prayers, Mae and I met in the staff room to discuss the previous night's incident and what discipline should be given to the staff. As we chatted, Mae suddenly exclaimed, "Why here they come now." A quick glance out the window revealed three soldiers of the Nigerian army striding purposefully toward the hospital office. They were in combat dress, but without weapons.

Both Mae and I assumed they had come to apologize. Mae met them on the walkway and invited them in. It rapidly became apparent they had not come to apologize, but to threaten us with a lawsuit. We had locked three soldiers of the Nigerian army in a room! We would be punished! We could not get a word in edgewise as they harangued us. Finally, I stood up and said, "This discussion is finished." I was surprised at their comments and angry with their insolence.

They followed me out of the office and by now their shouting had attracted a large number of staff and town's people. The soldiers were not finished and followed me until I stood with my back against the iron gate at the entrance to the hospital wards. They continued shouting and one of them shoved a number of papers into my face. Reflexively, my left hand came up striking his hand and scattering the papers all over the walkway. As the papers floated to the ground, the anger of the soldiers increased, and they whipped off their large army belts. My anger also increased.

Suddenly, a loud commanding voice rang out above the commotion. The soldiers immediately dropped their arms and walked meekly into the hospital compound. The colonel I had treated yesterday had observed the ruckus and was infuriated. The soldiers hung their heads under a merciless tongue lashing. They then crept off the grounds and returned to base.

"Better a patient person than a warrior, one with self-control than one who takes a city." (Proverbs 16:32) Have you ever lost your temper? That day I struggled with mine. In my own heart I believe the colonel's leg was broken so he could spare me, a young missionary doctor who momentarily forgot his Christian behavior and struggled with his temper. The Colonel's broken leg saved the doctor from the consequences of his anger.

PUNISHMENT?

*"You yourself will be very ill with a lingering
disease of the bowels, until the disease
causes your bowels to come out."*

2 CHRONICLES 21:15

Yesterday, a forty-six year old male arrived at the hospital. He had been carried on the heads of his two friends for at least twenty-five miles. They said he had noted a small soft mass in his right groin many years ago. Other than mild discomfort, it had been asymptomatic. Five days ago it became much larger and painful. Three days ago everything eaten or drank lead to violent episodes of vomiting.

On examination, his abdomen looked as if a large weather balloon had been blown up inside it. It was massively distended. Under the skin, loops of bowel were outlined and easily visible. On auscultation there were no bowel sounds. His skin was wet and sweaty. His heart was racing at greater than 180 beats per minute, and his blood pressure was undetectable. I was sure that the bowel had strangulated several days earlier.

In the "bush," our treatment of strangulated hernias was governed by a book called the *Companion to Surgery in West Africa.*

It had been written by two British surgeons many years before. They had dealt with many difficult surgical problems in Africa using only limited resources. First, the patient was put in the Trendelenburg position, which meant lowering the head below the feet to increase the blood flow to the heart. Then IV fluids were poured into the patient until the heart rate slowed to 100. A heart rate of 100 was the signal to attempt surgery. Finally, a nasogastric tube was inserted to begin the decompression of the dilated bowel and to empty its contents. Twelve hours later, the patient's pulse rate dropped to around 100, and he was passing small amounts of urine. We prepped him for surgery with little hope for survival. Survival is inversely proportional to the length of time the bowel has been strangulated. His bowel had been strangulated for 3 to 5 days.

The surgery was performed under local anesthetic, as the patient was too ill to attempt a general anesthetic. First the small bowel was severed near its gangrenous portion. This allowed the decompression of gas and fluid contents from the bowel. Then two feet of gangrenous bowel was removed and the bowel ends re-anastomosed. He tolerated the procedure well. IV fluids and antibiotics were continued for the next several days. Amazingly, he walked out of the hospital and rejoined his family two weeks later.

"You yourself will be very ill with a lingering disease of the bowels, until the disease causes your bowels to come out." (II Chronicles 21:15) This prophecy of Elijah was about the death of King Jehoram of Israel. It was God's punishment for his sinful reign. Are diseases God's punishment? They may be or they may be the consequences of a sinful lifestyle. I believe most diseases are simply the result of our birth into an imperfect, sinful world. We are born to die. Eternal life is promised only to those who have met God in Christ. Have you?

SELF-CONTROL

"But the fruit of the Spirit is love, joy, peace, forbearance, kindness, goodness, faithfulness, gentleness and self control..."

GALATIANS 5:22-23

When one is overworked and tired, it is easier to lose touch with the joy of Christian service. That day I arrived home from the hospital late for the evening meal. As Joan set the food before me, I began to relax. I relished the peace and quiet of home. However, before I could enjoy the meal, a quiet, apologetic voice sounded through the back screen door, "Gafara Likita, the police lorry has just brought a dead body for you to examine."

The body lay on the back of a large flat bed truck with slated wooden sides. When I arrived, a large crowd of villagers were pressing against the police standing around the vehicle. An officer informed me the body had been found in the "bush," and judging from its appearance and smell, it had lain there for several days. Almost all of us have seen the bloated dead body of an animal lying along the road. Dead bodies quickly swell, whether animal or human, from the action of bacteria; those left in the hot African sun do so even more quickly.

With some difficulty, I made my way through the crowd and climbed up on the truck. I was frustrated by the gawking crowd and the lack of any assistance with the body. The body was that of a large African male now bloated to over twice its normal size. The body was grotesquely swollen and the smell took one's breath away. There was matted blood and a blanket of flies covering the right side of the abdomen. It was nearly impossible to move the body alone. I was irritated and mumbled angrily to myself. I was irritated that no help was offered and that the body had been delivered so late in the day. Suddenly, an old African man peered up at me through the slats on the side of the truck. He pointed a finger at me and in an accusatory tone said, "And you call yourself a Christian." I was convicted to my core and to this day, whenever unjustifiable anger wells up within me, I can still clearly see his face and hand.

My anger was replaced with embarrassment at my poor witness. I elicited the help of several officers in dispersing the crowd. Then with the help of three other individuals, we carried the body to a secluded area on the hospital grounds. There under a tree, with the help of a surgical assistant, a partial autopsy was performed. In the fading sunlight, a cool breeze blew through the trees making the smell barely tolerable. An obvious gunshot wound, probably from a shotgun, had torn through the anterior abdomen. It perforated the bowel in many places before exciting through the back. The police had arrested a suspect.

It is so easy to feel justified in becoming angry. Yet anger is not a fruit of the Spirit. I should have been patient, gentle, and self-controlled. Do you ever lose your temper? Are you ever impatient? We never know who is observing us or who is turned away from our Christian faith by our loss of self-control or impatience

THE JUDGE

"For rulers hold no terror for those who do right,
but for those who do wrong. Do you want to be free
from fear of the one in authority? Then do
what is right and he will commend you."

ROMANS 13:3

A month after the autopsy, I was called to testify in the Federal High Court in Makurdi.

Nigeria was a former British colony and it's system of justice is modeled after the British system. I was flown to Makurdi on a mission plane and found a car waiting for me at the airfield. I was quickly driven to the courthouse.

Once inside the courtroom, I was immediately led to the witness box. I was not fully prepared for the incongruity of the setting. The front of the courtroom was richly paneled in hardwoods with the judge's bench some three feet off the floor. The floor was, however, of dirt and there was no glass in the small windows. Beneath the windows children played and their voices were clearly audible. The courthouse was of typical bush construction with the dirt floor and a tin roof. I guess I had expected something a bit more substantial.

The bailiff's loud voice quickly drew my attention back to the front of the courtroom as the judge entered. There on the bench sat a coal-black African, arrayed in a small white powdered wig and an elaborate red robe. I had to suppress a smile as I glanced first at the dirt floor beneath me and then back to "His Lordship" as the judge was to be addressed. I am not sure what he thought of my midwestern accent, but he spoke with impeccable Oxford articulation and certainly spoke the King's English better than I. Despite his austere appearance, he was pleasant and friendly. He treated me with deference and warned the lawyers not to waste my time.

My testimony was quite straightforward detailing the results of the autopsy. There were but a few questions from the defense and prosecuting attorneys, and the judge quickly excused me. I was brought back to the airport and immediately returned to Takum.

Do you fear those in authority? "...Then do what is right and he will commend you. (Romans 13:3) This may not always happen, but it is what God expects from those He places in authority. Those who do no wrong should not be afraid of those in authority. Pray for judges who recognize their authority comes from God.

THANKFULNESS

*"May this water that brings a curse enter your body
so that your abdomen swells and your thigh wastes
away. or your womb miscarries..."*

NUMBERS 5:22

This passage from the Old Testament was in reference
to a curse placed upon unfaithful wives. In Africa, this
"curse" was more commonly seen among those suffering
from extra pulmonary tuberculosis, in this case, tuberculosis
of the peritoneum or abdomen.

The young Fulani woman was about thirty years old and
had been ill for the past several months. Her arms and legs
were very thin and wasted from disease. Her abdomen was
swollen beyond belief. It was massive, extending at least three
feet or more in front of her and covering her below the knees
when seated. She was in a great deal of pain from the massive
fluid carried in the abdomen and could not walk or stand
without assistance.

Further examination, including a chest x-ray, failed to
reveal tuberculosis in the lungs. Her skin test for TB was,
however, positive. A sample of the abdominal fluid was

removed with a needle and syringe. This was sent to a pathology laboratory in the United States. Unless tubercular bacteria were seen on a smear, it would be weeks before we had a definitive diagnosis. The patient could be dead by then. On the basis of her positive skin test, I began empiric treatment for peritoneal tuberculosis.

The patient pleaded with me for the removal of all of the fluid from her abdomen. For her, the pain and immobility were becoming intolerable. She had been suffering for months. It was difficult for her to understand, that although I could easily remove the fluid, it would rapidly re-accumulate. The removal might take her life because of the enormous loss of body proteins in the fluid. I begged her to trust me and as a compromise, removed about a gallon of the fluid. She then agreed to continue the tuberculosis medication and realized it would be weeks for improvement to occur.

Thankfully, she responded to the tubercular therapy. First the ascites stabilized and the abdomen no longer increased in size. She began to gain weight and strength. Slowly, over two months the fluid resolved. She was profusely grateful for the care and promised to finish the medications we sent home with her.

The parade of horrendous disease and suffering among my African patients taught me I had nothing to complain about; yet how often Christians complain. When you are tempted to complain remember all that God has done for you. If that is not enough, thank Him for all the things you do not have, but with which others are afflicted. You will realize you have nothing to complain about, only thankfulness.

DAD

*"Cast all your anxiety on him
because he cares for you."*

1 PETER 5:7

I received several letters from my parents over the past few months that have greatly concerned me. My father had not felt well and had lost nearly thirty pounds. A few weeks vacation with his brother in Florida did nothing to restore his health or strength. I told him by letter that he needed a second opinion and further testing. It was at times like this that our isolation from the family was most difficult.

This week I received a letter from Dr. Harv Bratt; he was the surgeon who gave me the crash course in general surgery when I first arrived on the field. Further testing on my Dad revealed both an active gastric ulcer and a localized malignancy in his stomach. Harv took him to surgery and found no apparent metastatic disease. These tumors were, however, highly unpredictable. I wished I could return home to be with him. That, of course, was impossible with the physician shortage here in Africa.

As I reflected on my parents and my dad's battle with cancer, I wrote the following letter:

"You and Mom have had a full life together. There have been joys, sorrows, and great pain when brother Peter was killed during World War II. Raising a family of six boys certainly must have had its frustrations, but also great joys and accomplishments. We each in a special way contributed to the problems and heartaches, but also to the joys and accomplishments. Now we all have sons and daughters of our own to raise.

I know that I speak for all of us when I say we have had a wonderful Christian home, full of love and deep family unity. It has given each of us a solid foundation for homes and families of our own. We love you both dearly and trust you realize how much you have meant and mean to us. Naturally, we hope your life will be spared for some time Dad, for Mom, for yourself, and for all of us. Our family particularly, so far away and gone already for so long, wishes to have time with you once again. The thought of not seeing you this side of heaven is not a joyful one, and we selfishly pray that God will spare you. In any case, we pray for the grace to accept God's will, whatever that may be."

My father was to live another two years before dying of his gastric cancer. God allowed us to spend nearly a year with him after our return from Africa.

Are you ever anxious? Is your life burdened with care and frustration? "Cast all your anxiety on Him because he cares for you." (1 Peter 5:7) Prayer, petition, and thanksgiving are the Christian's answer to fear and anxiety. Do you practice it daily?

BURNED

"You have filled my heart with greater joy than
when their grain and new wine abound."

PSALM 4:7

A fifteen-year-old Fulani boy was carried into the hospital by his father and older brother. Two months ago he had been making homemade gun powder when it exploded. He suffered a deep burn extending from his left anterior thigh up to and including the left side of his abdomen and lower chest. The burn had healed by scarring until his left thigh was now scarred tightly against the left side of his chest. It was a severe flexion contraction.

Through an interpreter, I explained to the father that we could help him, but it would be a long process. I would have to cut away all of the scar tissue and free his leg, otherwise he would never walk again. The father agreed, and the next day the young boy was taken to surgery. Removal of the scar tissue resulted in a large, open, raw wound from his left nipple to just above his left knee. After dressing the wound, I put the boy to bed. The left leg was wrapped to a 2x12 board to keep the leg from flexing back onto the chest.

His dressings were changed twice a day while we waited for granulation tissue. Each morning on rounds, I watched carefully for any signs of infection. The young boy did not comprehend what I was trying to do. He knew that although his leg was nearly straight, he now had a painful open wound and his leg was tied uncomfortably to a large board. He cursed me freely in Fulani at every visit. My nurse interpreters would smile, and give me the sanitized version. Fortunately, I knew few Fulani words and those were not the most colorful and descriptive. However, his anger was clear.

A few days later, I was able to take him back to surgery. With an old Brown dermatome, I was able to harvest enough split thickness skin from his other leg and the right side of the abdomen to cover the open wound. Ten days later there was minimal infection and at least 70 percent of the skin graft had taken. Slowly over many more days the skin filled in the remaining raw areas. He finally understood what had been done and the cursing stopped. With physical therapy, he began to stand and then took his first faltering steps. Soon he was ready for discharge. I walked with him out of the hospital to his waiting father. Suddenly, he knelt down and taking both of my hands in his, he kissed them. His gratitude more than erased the anger and curses he had previously directed at me.

" You have filled my heart with greater joy…" (Psalm 4:7) My young burn patient's heart was filled with joy as he walked out of the hospital. The Psalmist is telling us that God has filled the very center of our being with joy. Are you experiencing that joy? Are you a joy- filled Christian?

FISHERMEN

"'Come follow me', Jesus said, 'and
I will make you fishers of men.'"

MATTHEW 4:19

D r. Ed Stehouwer arrived in Takum this past week; he had been on the mission field for many years and was the physician I replaced. As I had spent most of the past 1-1/2 years alone, he had returned to help out for the next six weeks. This not only gave me some relief from the hospital work, but it allowed me to leave the mission compound. Joan and I hoped to get away for a few days visiting outlying clinics and perhaps a bit of vacation.

Last Friday I drove the 150 miles to Serti with several of the other missionaries. We spent a night on the river and returned late Saturday. It was an opportunity to fish for one of the largest freshwater fish in the world. It is called the Nile perch or in Hausa, Giwan Rua, "the elephant of the water." It can grow to six feet in length and nearly 500 pounds or more.

The river was over sixty feet wide and flowed swiftly. In many places it was very deep and was inhabited by hippopotamus and crocodiles. We were told it was safe to swim here as the predators preferred quieter portions of the river.

As there were no bridges, one had to swim to get to the other side. I was amazed how quickly I could swim with one hand while carrying a fishing pole in the other. I am sure imagining one of those reptiles beneath me sped my progress.

Two of the missionaries hooked smaller versions of the Nile perch, and we saw them as they leaped out of the water. Unfortunately, they also escaped the hooks. None of the rest of us even had a bite. In the gathering darkness, we took refuge on a large sandbar in the middle of the river. We set up camp there with a large fire for both warmth and cooking. I was surprised how cold it became at night sleeping in the open. We all nestled closer and closer to the fire, keeping at least one side warm. I was rudely awakened when one of my tennis shoes caught fire.

In the morning, Ray Prins hooked a monster fish that broke his line and took the lure. Although I caught nothing, I really enjoyed the fellowship and two days away from the hospital stresses.

Some missionaries returned several weeks later and hit the jackpot. They caught thirty of the fish, each weighing 35 to 45 pounds. They brought them back in a pickup truck and shared them with everyone on three mission compounds. Deep-fried,,they were as good as the perch from Lake Michigan, only these fillets were huge.

"'Come follow me', Jesus said, 'and I will make you fishers of men…'" (Matthew 4:19) Do you like to fish? There are many members of our churches, both male and female, who love fishing. They will spend large sums of money, endure hardships, and spend hours of their time in the effort to catch a fish. How many of you like to share your faith? Jesus called us to be fishers of men. How much money, time, and effort do you put into it?

SERVANTS

"For we do not preach ourselves,
but Jesus Christ as Lord, and ourselves
as your servants for Jesus' sake."

2 CORINTHIANS 4:5

While Dr. Stehouwer covered the hospital, Joan and I, along with the family, visited various medical clinics. We drove over two hundred miles in three days. That doesn't seem far, but we averaged less than twenty miles an hour on the rutted dirt roads. The medical assistants were eager to show their abilities and a large number of patients were seen. Needless to say, we were eager to be home after three days on the road.

Passing through one of the villages sixty miles from Takum, we stopped briefly to rest and chat with the villagers. A full three-and-a-half hours later, we arrived on the outskirts of Takum. We were all tired, dirty, and thirsty. Rounding the final curve, we were stopped by a small boy waving frantically at the side of the road. Joan rolled down the window and he excitedly gushed, "Likita, my grandfather is very sick and needs a doctor." "Where is your grandfather," I asked. He then informed me he was in the village we had passed through over three hours before.

I dropped Joan and the children off at our home. Quickly freshening up, I filled another bottle with water and checked the gas tank. Then I retraced the trip made earlier that afternoon. I was grumpy alone in the car, wondering why we hadn't been told about this patient when we were in the village around noon. I grumbled to myself the entire three hour trip. Reaching the village in early evening, I was taken to the old man's hut. It was obvious he had been ill for a long time and was dying. He was skin and bones with a hard mass protruding from his abdomen. I had a pleasant conversation with him and his family. The grandfather had no interest in returning with me to the hospital. I agreed, because the long ride would have been painful and there was little I could do for him. I explained he would probably die soon and left pain medicine for him. I arrived home late that night.

I did not sleep well. Although I had returned and was pleasant with the patient, my anger and attitude about returning was wrong. After the morning worship service, we sat down for lunch. Joan had no sooner placed the food on the table when there was a knock on the back door. As I walked toward the screen door, a young man said, "Likita, my mother is very ill in the bush and you need to come with the car." As I opened the door God touched my heart. I was clearly reminded that I had promised God I would go and would do whatever He wanted. I smiled and grabbed the car keys.

How do you serve others? Do you serve with joy, begrudgingly, or with excuses? It is very easy to promise God that you will go wherever He wants and do whatever He asks. It is quite another thing to do so with a joyful heart as servants for Christ's sake. Remember, that servants do not choose the time, place, or convenience of service. They simply obey with a joyful heart.

ONLY HUMAN

*"As Peter entered the house, Cornelius met
him and fell at his feet in reverence.
But Peter made him get up. 'Stand up,' he said,
'I am only a man myself.'"*

ACTS 10:25-26

Today, several colleagues and I shared a unique experience. It has been just over five months since the Aku Uka died at our hospital. Today the Jukun elders will choose a new god and king. For centuries this selection has been done in secret, under the same sacred tree. This year, perhaps in response to the international news surrounding the Aku's death at Takum hospital, portions of the ceremony were opened. Invitations were given to the Nigerian press, the film industry, and several government dignitaries. Five missionaries were also invited.

We arrived in Wukari early in the morning and were led by Jukun guides deep into the forest. Along the way we passed many silent sentinels stationed on tall rocks and behind trees. Some carried spears and a few had shotguns, while others had only knives. Most were dressed in animal skins with parts of their bodies and faces fiercely painted. Finally, we were motioned to sit down on one side of the trail.

Standing, we could see a bit further into the forest. There ahead of us, in a small clearing, stood an old, large, stately tree. On either side of the trail, twenty or more Jukun men lay prostrate; each was dressed only in a white skirt, with bare feet, and was naked from the waist up. Their hair was braided in a double queue at the back of their heads. Soon a procession of tribal leaders passed us and walked between those lying on the ground. These men were also naked from the waist up but wore brightly colored skirts. The skirts markedly contrasted with the white skirts of those now lying face down in the dust. Their hair was also braided in a double queue. These men were known as the "Kingmakers."

Thirty minutes later, a lone male, his head wrapped with a long bright red scarf, passed us. His body was covered with a long cloak made of stripes of orange, red, and black cloth. With one hand, he held the bridle of a bareback white horse, which he lead quickly toward those gathered under the tree. Moments later, with much shouting and excitement, the Kingmakers raced toward us. Astride the white horse, in the middle of the Kingmakers, rode the new Aku Uka. Behind him on the horse rode the mummified remains of the previous Aku. He was dressed in the royal robes of his office with his arms tied around the waist of the new leader. Ostensibly, this was his final ride to the land of the god's. The Jukun people believed the Aku Uka's were neither born nor died.

"As Peter entered the house, Cornelius met him and fell at his feet in reverence. But Peter made him get up. 'Stand up', he said, 'I am only a man myself.'" Acts 10:25-26 It was an honor to see this centuries old secret tradition. It was sad to see people worshiping another human being as god. Today, many still "worship" leaders and celebrities as if they were gods. Do you? Stand up; they are only men and women like yourself.

HEART FAILURE

"There in front of him was a man suffering
from dropsy... So taking hold of the man,
he healed him and sent him on his way."

LUKE 14:2, 4

T he patient, a wealthy businessman, had traveled many
miles to see us. For the past ten years he had endured the
pain and discomfort of huge bilateral hernias. When I saw
him I could hardly believe my eyes and ears. His breathing
was labored, and I found both of his lungs were partially filled
with fluid. He had two large edematous scrotal hernias. Both
of his legs were grossly swollen with fluid from his waist to his
feet. There was so much fluid in the skin that my examining
finger disappeared when pressed into it. He not only had two
hernias, but also was suffering from severe dropsy. Today it is
called congestive heart failure.

I explained to the patient that I could not operate on
his hernias until the problem with his heart was corrected. I
suspected a recent heart attack, but had neither blood tests nor
an EKG machine to confirm my suspicions. I admitted him
to the hospital and began diuretics and Digoxin to correct his

florid heart failure. Within three weeks he lost over seventy pounds and both looked and felt ten years younger. He was no longer short of breath, and his lungs were clear. He was discharged to live in the town for several weeks to gain further strength. He was instructed to continue his medication, to eat a banana daily for its potassium, and to eat very little salt.

When he returned for surgery, he had lost another ten pounds. At surgery a relaxing incision was first made in the abdominal wall. This allowed expansion and enabled me to push all of his small intestines from the hernia sacs back into his abdominal cavity. The hernias were then repaired. He tolerated the procedure without difficulty and there was no return of his congestive heart failure. The patient was now barely recognizable as the man who presented at the hospital over seven weeks previously. He was delighted!

On discharge, the need to continue a low salt diet for life was stressed. He was encouraged to continue his medication as well as the daily banana. If he could not return to Takum, he must see another physician to monitor his heart and medications.

"There in front of Him was a man suffering from dropsy...." Luke 14:2 A man with a heart problem, so Jesus healed him. Few of us suffer from dropsy, but all of us have a heart problem— the problem of sin. A problem no physician can heal. "What can wash away my sins? Nothing but the blood of Jesus." Have you been washed? Is there now any comparison to the man or woman you used to be?

MORE THAN MEDICINE

*"And not to steal from them, but to show
they can be fully trusted, so that in every way
they will make the teaching about
God our Savior attractive."*

TITUS 2:10

The Greys have finally returned to Takum, and next month a third doctor, Dr. John Channer, will join us. He had just completed a surgical residency. We will finally have a full complement of physicians. With help at hand I could now pursue other interests with a bit more freedom and time. I had enjoyed preaching and had conducted services once a month and occasionally more often in the past.

Last night was a special experience for me. I had been invited to be the opening speaker for a women's fellowship meeting in the village of Kwambi. The eight mile motorcycle ride under a full tropical moon was in itself delightful. At the village, over two hundred women had gathered. They would spend the next two days together. Five times each day they met for Bible study and instruction. The days were long, beginning at 6:00 a.m. and not ending until 9:30 p.m.

The enthusiasm and singing of the ladies was contagious. I thoroughly enjoyed it. I sang vigorously along with them, but in English not Kutev. Their enthusiasm increased mine as I delivered the message from the letter of the Apostle Paul to Titus. The first ten verses of the second chapter deal with instructions on character and Christian living. Characteristics, the apostle Paul states, that will make the gospel attractive to others. I really preferred the old King James Version that states we "adorn" the gospel. Thus making the gospel more beautiful and appealing by the living testimony of our lives.

The message was well received. I hoped my surgical assistant was able to translate my exegesis of the passage into the Kutev language. I had often been frustrated by my inability to share my faith with patients and friends here. Medical necessity did not allow me time for language study and the lack of another physician crimped my opportunities for anything other than the practice of medicine.

"...So that in every way they will make the teaching about God our Savior more attractive..." (Titus 2:10 What do you think is said about your character? Is your life a living sacrifice acceptable to God? Do you feel your life "..makes the teaching about God... more attractive" or does it cause those who observe it to pause or question your Christian faith?

FISH

*"For everything God created is good,
and nothing is to be rejected if it is received
with thanksgiving, because it is consecrated
by the word of God and prayer."*

1 TIMOTHY 4:4-5

Last week I flew to a medical clinic in the village of Ibi. Ibi is a large village on the southern bank of the Benue River, one of Nigeria's largest rivers. I spent nearly the entire day working with the medical assistant. He met me at the airstrip and took me first to the home of the village chief. Although a Muslim, he was very friendly to the Christian missionaries. He appreciated our medical work and midwife services. He gladly granted me permission to see patients that day.

While visiting, one of the chief's men butchered a goat in a corner of the compound. Before we left, the chief ordered him to give me a portion of the goat's liver and lung. Both were considered an honor to receive. I thanked him and after leaving gave the meat to the medical attendant's wife for our lunch.

We saw patients for several hours before returning to his home. His wife had prepared a fish miya for us. This is like a stew. It also contained the liver and lung I had received that morning. It was very good. I did, however, feel slightly squeamish about the portions of unclean fish. Scales had been removed, it was cooked, but the entrails were clearly visible in each cross-sectioned piece of fish. The liver was tasty, but the lung was more like chewing on a sponge.

Ibi is a well-known fishing village because of its location on the Benue River. In mid- afternoon, I went down to the market and purchased fifty pounds of fish to carry back to the missionaries at Takum. Fresh fish was a treat in the bush, and we did not often get it. Unlike the Africans, I first had to clean them. Two of the fisherman helped me with the cleaning, amidst a great deal of laughter. They hooted and joked together as the pile of heads and entrails grew. Although, I could not understand their comments, I knew that they and the others were laughing at the white man's foolishness. Foolishly throwing away the best parts of the fish! The entrails and severed heads were given to the local pastor. He was deeply appreciative of the gift and his wife soon added them to their stew.

"For everything God created is good, and nothing is to be rejected if it is received with thanksgiving…" (I Timothy 4:4) Often I and other missionaries were served food that would not be eaten in our own culture. Here we have the luxury of choosing what we will eat, whereas the African accepted whatever was available and wasted nothing. They were thankful and content with what they had. Are you content with what God has given you? Even more importantly, are you thankful?

NIGHT FLIGHT

"Neither do people light a lamp and put it
under a bowl. Instead they put it on its stand,
and it gives light to everyone in the house."

MATTHEW 5:15

Ray Browneye arrived at the airstrip in Ibi around 4:30 p.m. We then flew to Mkar to pick up two other passengers, Ray Prins and his wife, Phyllis. All of us saw the darkening sky, and in the distance a large thunderstorm was forming. It appeared to be in the area of Takum, some eighty miles away. After some discussion, Ray decided it would still be safe to fly to Takum rather than spending the night here in Mkar. With forty pounds of cleaned fresh fish, I was delighted we could continue the flight home. By now it was nearly 6:00 p.m.

We were quickly airborne. However, by the time we had crossed the river at Harga, the rain was coming down in sheets and the plane was bucking and bouncing in the heavy winds. In the distance, dark clouds now obscured Takum mountain and the sky around us rolled with black menacing clouds. Loud thunder periodically vibrated through the plane, while the darkness was intermittently pierced with streaks of lightening. To avoid straying too close to the now unseen mountain, Ray searched for the Harga road and lowered the plane's altitude to less than two-hundred feet. Dimly visible beneath us was the dirt road from Harga to Takum. It was now our flight path.

The wind and rain continually buffeted the small aircraft, and we bounced up and down above the dirt roadway beneath. By the time we approached Takum, night had fallen. The storm clouds obscured any light from the moon or stars. The airstrip, which lay beyond the mission compound, like the countryside around it, was enveloped in darkness. Ray directed the plane toward the airstrip. Through the windshield a tiny point of light was barely discernible. Ray's wife, Ann, hearing the plane's approach, had lit a kerosene lantern. She then raced to the middle of the airstrip and stood at the end nearest the approaching plane. Holding the lantern above her head, she provided a target and altitude above the runway for Ray. With the skill that came from countless previous landings, he put us safely down on the airstrip in the pitch darkness. The landing was uneventful with the exception of a reprimand and fine from the local police for landing after dark.

"Neither do people light a lamp and put it under a bowl. Instead they put it on its stand, and it gives light to everyone in the house." (Matthew 5:15) Jesus wasn't referring to the kerosene lantern Ann provided in the darkness. He was referring to the light each of us is to provide with our lives in a sin-darkened world. "This little light of mine. I am going to let it shine." Do you?

TRADITIONS

*"I was advancing in Judaism beyond many
of my own age and was extremely zealous
for the traditions of my fathers."*

GALATIANS 1:14

J oan and I returned from Jos today after a brief four day vacation. I was immediately greeted at the airport with some very sad news. While I was in Jos, one of our hospital nurses had died. He had a brief illness lasting only a few days. He had apparently become ill the day we left. Now he was already dead. Malam Ibraham Musa was only twenty-nine years old and left behind a young wife and a child. He had worked for several years at the hospital. Over the past two years, we had become fast friends. In addition to working together, we played tennis nearly every week. I deeply miss him and his visits to our home where he frequently stopped, just to talk.

Although he had been hospitalized immediately, the course of his disease was rapidly downhill. He had been jaundiced on admission and became comatose the following day. The rapid course and characteristics of his death made us suspect that he had taken a native remedy called "Magani Shewara." I had never seen a patient with hepatitis survive this native remedy. It is a concoction of cow's urine mixed with native herbs. The witch doctors administer it to all patients with jaundice. Ibraham knew about the toxic effects of this medicine, having himself cared for many of its victims. However, family pressures and tribal traditions to take the medicine are so strong that few can resist. As is the custom in the tropics, he was buried within a few hours of his death.

Yesterday, Joan and I went to greet his wife, child, and family. Ibraham was a Christian and I knew that his larger family would continue to care for his wife and child. Among the pagans the widow was frequently sent away, while the children become the property of the decedents brother or father. We arrived to find many people still gathered both inside and outside his home. Africans mourn and show their grief simply by their presence. Sometimes they will sit with family members for days during which little is said. Their presence conveying the grief they shared.

"I was advancing in Judaism beyond many of my own age among my people and was extremely zealous for the traditions of my fathers." (Galatians 1:14) All families and cultures have traditions. Some indeed are very zealously guarded. The tradition of Ibraham's family cost him his life. Do you blindly follow traditions of your family or church? Or are you willing to evaluate traditions that interfere with the love of Christ in relation to others?

SCHOOL

"Fathers, do not exasperate your children;
instead, bring them up in the training
and instruction of the Lord."

EPHESIANS 6:4

J oan brought a number of books to Africa with the hope of home schooling Christy. In 1970 there were few, if any, home study programs available. Christy had a mind of her own and was unable to concentrate for the length of time her mother wished. It was frustrating for both and home schooling soon fell to the wayside as an educational option. Christy was very intelligent and already reading. She needed stimulation and direction from someone other than her mother. Rather than continually frustrating her, the decision to send her to boarding school several hundred miles away was made. It was difficult for us.

Christy, on the other hand, seemed eager to go. She was sure it would be great fun. Joan really wanted to keep Christy home with the family. However, with the failure of home schooling, boarding school was now our only other option. The separation would be difficult. Joan quickly finished the clothing she had sewn for the school year. Not only would Christy need extra clothing, but also each piece must have her name sewn inside for the school laundry.

This morning Christy left for school. As she waited to board the airplane, it was as difficult for her as for her parents. She had been so eager to go, but now the realization that she would be going without Mom, Dad, or siblings was hitting home. She tried to put on a brave face. However, the picture taken by the camera reveals a sad little girl struggling to hold back her tears. We hugged and kissed and then said goodbye. Her mother cried openly as did her brother Tim.

We have met her house-parents and know they will help her in adjusting to life away from home. It will be hardest for Joan and Tim, as she has been their constant companion. Fortunately, all students are required to write a letter home once a week. Christy's first letter home left Mom a bit more confident with the separation. Much later, Christy confided that she cried nearly every night.

"Fathers (and mothers), do not exasperate your children; instead, bring them up in the training and instruction of the Lord." (Ephesians 6:4) Children must obey and honor their parents. Parents on the other hand must not needlessly anger, frustrate, or exasperate their children. We are not only to discipline them, but also to love them in a Christ-like way. That includes apologizing and asking for forgiveness when we make errors in parenting. Does your parenting frustrate your child? Does he or she frustrate you? Do you respond appropriately?

BURDENS

"Carry each other's burdens, and in this way
you will fulfill the law of Christ."

GALATIANS 6:2

A great burden for many in Africa is the problem of elephantiasis. This disease deforms the patient for life. The grotesque deformities that result often cause social alienation and make it difficult to earn a living. Any dependent part of the body is at risk including arms, legs, breasts, and scrotums. It is caused by the bite of a mosquito carrying the larva of a worm that causes lymphatic filariasis. The adult worms live for many years in the body. They are about four inches in length and during their life cycle obstruct the lymphatic drainage systems. This results in enormous permanent swelling of limbs and genitalia.

Most commonly, pictures are seen of lower extremities with elephantiasis. The limbs are often swollen 2 to 4 time's normal size. Over time, the skin becomes thickened, rough, and dry. It resembles the leg of an elephant, hence its name. The skin cracks frequently leading to severe secondary bacterial infections and many times death. A month ago a young women presented with a grossly swollen right breast. Its weight would not allow her to stand erect but forced her to walk bent in half. The breast was amputated and weighed over twenty-five pounds. But she was now free and could walk in a normal position.

Elephantiasis was seen nearly daily at the hospital. There is no treatment once the worms have died and scarred the lymphatic system. During my years in Africa, eighteen young men presented with severe elephantiasis of the scrotum. They wanted surgical modification as they were planning on marriage. Their scrotums hung well below their knees and weighed more than 40 pounds. Often they had improvised a walking aid, a small narrow wheelbarrow on which the scrotum rested. The functional disability was enormous as were the problems of mobility.

Each patient was taken to surgery to undergo a surgical procedure known as a scrotal-plasty. The majority of the edematous tissue was removed and a smaller scrotum fashioned from remaining skin. Usually, this required removal of one testicle as well. However, one remaining testicle allowed for progeny.

"Carry each other's burdens, and in this way you will fulfill the law of Christ." (Galatians 6:2) There are burdens everywhere. Few of you will ever have to deal with elephantiasis, but how about those individuals carrying the burdens of poverty, sickness, divorce, loneliness, depression, and hunger? Do you ever see anyone carrying these burdens? Do you know someone carrying such a burden? What are you doing to ease or help them?

HELPERS

"...I urge you brothers and sisters,
to submit to such as these and to everyone
who joins in the work and labors at it.

1 CORINTHIANS 16:15-16

The Channer family has finally arrived in Takum! We now have three doctors for the first time since I have been here. It will be short lived, however, as the Channers will take six months of language study in Kano once a teacher is available. Then Herm and I will be alone until our furlough.

I quickly took advantage of having a trained surgeon at Takum. It happened on his first night here. In the early morning, I was called to the hospital to see a young Jukun woman who had just been carried in by neighbors. Earlier that day she had been climbing a palm tree harvesting palm oil nuts. She slipped while climbing high in the tree and fell toward the ground. Her body was impaled on a smaller tree. A branch, three inches in diameter, penetrated through her body. It entered through her right posterior chest and exited just below the left breast. Other villagers sawed through the branch to free her from the tree. Wisely, they had not tried to remove the branch. Miraculously, she was still alive.

As we prepped the patient for surgery, I sent one of my assistants to get Dr. Channer out of bed. I was not worried about his sleep as much as this difficult case. He might as well get his feet wet. Together, we removed the large branch from her chest cavity. After cleaning all the debris from the chest, we partially closed her wounds and inserted a chest tube. We arranged for appropriate drainage. We then explored her swollen abdomen and removed the blood found there. Further examination revealed a small laceration of the liver as the cause of bleeding. The branch had also lacerated her liver as it penetrated her body. We stopped the bleeding with gel foam and then closed the abdomen.

The patient did remarkably well and her right lung fully expanded. Antibiotics controlled the infection and her chest tube was removed a week later. Two pints of blood, donated by friends, markedly improved her condition. I was relaxed as we did this difficult surgery together. Finally, someone else made the difficult decisions and gave input as to the best way to proceed.

"I urge you, brothers and sisters,...to submit to everyone who joins in the work and labors at it." (I Corinthians 16:15-16) You cannot do it alone, on the mission field, in the church, or in your lives. We all need help from others. The Apostle Paul likened Christians to a body with many members and different gifts. All are necessary and all contribute. Do you gladly accept the contributions of others? Do you appreciate those working with you?

UNSEEN

*"Do not boast about tomorrow, for you
do not know what a day may bring."*

PROVERBS 27:1

Yesterday the family and I flew to Serti. I was scheduled to supervise the maternity center that week while the nurse midwife had a short vacation. Serti is about a two hour flight from Takum, 150 miles to the southeast. The village lies in a valley surrounded by mountains. Joan and I, along with the pilot, Gord Buys, and our two small children, filled the small single-engine airplane to capacity.

The sky was clear, with bright sunshine and unlimited visibility when we left Takum. We were totally unprepared for what awaited us at Serti. The sky above the clouds was still clear and bright but the valley looked as if clouds of cool whip had been poured into it. Only the tips of the mountains surrounding the valley were visible. I had flown years before in the USAF under similar conditions. Then an air-controller guided us to the unseen runway by radio and radar. Flights in the bush are by compass, direct visualization, and experience, because there are no control towers, radios, or radar.

The village of Serti and the runway were totally obscured by the opaque layer of clouds. For the next thirty minutes, Gord guided the plane as we dove in and out of the clouds searching for the airstrip. Once through the thick cloud layer, we flew at tree top level frantically searching for the airstrip in the less dense ground fog. Each attempt was brief, limited by our lack of visibility in the fog and the mountains tightly surrounding the valley. The end of each search was clearly signaled by the screaming aircraft engine as it lifted us up and free of the clouds once more.

Unseen below us, nearly the entire population of Serti along with the soldiers garrisoned there, were gathering by the airstrip. Each was drawn by the screaming sounds of the unseen aircraft repeatedly diving and climbing through the dense cloud layer above them. On the next attempt, we caught a fleeting glance of the airstrip nestled beside the trees. We climbed out of the clouds once more before diving back to a safe landing. It had been a harrowing end to what we had expected to be a pleasant flight. We offered a prayer of thanks in the cockpit, adding it to the countless prayers offered silently during the past thirty minutes.

"Do not boast about tomorrow, for you do not know what a day may bring." (Proverbs 27:1) Do you boast about tomorrow? Do you worry about tomorrow? God has mercifully left tomorrow unseen. We should not boast of what we might do or steal the joys of today by our fears of tomorrow. We need to only trust our lives to the hands of a faithful Savior.

FROGS

"If you refuse to let them go, I will send a plague
of frogs on your whole country... but when
Pharaoh saw that there was relief, he hardened
his heart and would not listen to Moses
and Aaron, just as the Lord had said."

EXODUS 8:2, 15

Each rainy season, for about a week, the land here is infested with frogs. The frogs reminded me of the Biblical story of the plagues of Egypt. The amphibians hibernated underground and after the heavy rains began, they suddenly appear everywhere. They were not of Biblical proportions, but one could hardly walk without stepping on them. I felt badly, when the nightly trips to the hospital were punctuated by the popping sounds as frogs were crushed under the wheels of my motorcycle. They literally covered the road and were impossible to avoid.

Some ultimately found their way into the house and had to be escorted outside. One pesky fellow took up residence in our toilet. Nightly we were awakened by the sounds of splashing in the bathroom. Unable to sleep, I shone a flashlight into the room and found the frog perched on the slippery slope of the bowl. It was unable to jump out of the toilet but continually slipped back into the water. When I drew closer, it dove into the water and disappeared in the outlet pipe. After several nightly awakenings, I finally put a little bowl cleaner into the water. The frog did not return.

An occasional frog in the house was not a major problem. However, frogs were also an attraction as well as a popular food for snakes. We were afraid of the poisonous snakes and certainly did not want them in the house. Then suddenly, almost overnight, the frogs were gone not to return for another year.

"If you refuse to let them go, I will send a plague of frogs on your whole country ...but when Pharaoh saw that there was relief, he hardened his heart and would not listen to Moses and Aaron, just as the Lord had said." (Exodus 8:2,15) When one reads the story of the plagues of Egypt, you are struck by how compliant Pharaoh becomes under the stress of each plague. Then how quickly he forgets what he had promised after the plague is gone. Do you only pray when you have needs or problems? Do you forget about God after He has answered your needs or relieved the problem? You need a daily interaction with Him. You need to daily give Him praise and express your thankfulness. Don't just call on Him when you are in trouble.

SACRIFICES

"Therefore, I urge you brothers and sisters,
in view of God's mercy, to offer your bodies
as living sacrifices, holy and pleasing to God—
this is your spiritual act of worship."

ROMANS 12:1

Takum Christian Hospital
December 1, 1970

Dear Christian Friends, the rains have long since ceased and the trees and grasses are rapidly turning brown. The leaves are falling from the trees and the air is filled with the heavy dust carried by the Harmattan winds. Like the first snowfall of winter, these signs remind us that another year is drawing to a close. Not only the end of the year for our family, but the end of our term of service here in Nigeria.

Two-and-a-half years at times seems like yesterday. When we look at our changing family, it is apparent that many yesterdays have passed. Christy has grown into a young lady and is attending school at Hillcrest. Tim is no longer a toddler but a husky lad proud of his abilities at riding a two wheeled bike. Debra is nearly a year old and was not even in the family plans when we arrived in Nigeria. It really has been two-and-a-half years. We have all changed and grown a bit older, and we trust this has been toward a richer and more meaningful Christian life.

Each of us, at home or on the mission field, is called to be a servant for Christ's sake. Offering ourselves as living sacrifices. For my family and I this term of service has provided new insights into just what Christ may require of us. Like the amazed disciples when Jesus washed their feet, we too had but an inkling of the depth and responsibility of being a servant for His sake. We have been blessed and are grateful for His guidance over the past years. For accomplishments we give thanks. For shortcomings and failures we ask pardon and grace to begin anew. We have been blessed by our African brothers and sisters and we trust we have been a blessing to them.

We would encourage your continued prayers and support for the mission work here in Nigeria. The seed has been sown for many years and the harvest is plentiful. Pray that the members of the African church may be filled with a desire and willingness to live a Christian life and proclaim the gospel to those who have not heard.

May you have a blessed Christmas with God's richest blessings now and in the coming New Year. May you have real joy and peace in your heart and an increased dedication of your life.

"Therefore I urge you brothers and sisters...to offer your bodies as living a sacrifice..." (Romans 12:1) What does God require of you? He requires not only your faith and belief, but also the activities of your life. Is your life a living sacrifice?

FAREWELL

"When they asked him to spend more time with them,
he declined. But as he left, he promised,
'I will come back if it is God's will'..."

ACTS 18:20-21

Last week we were honored by the village of Kwambi. The church there has been our home church and where I have served as an elder since arriving on the mission field. Little Debra was baptized there a few months ago. I rode out to the village in the morning to see what was expected of my family and I. We were to be the guests of honor and would be seated in front of the entire village. There would be a full meal and farewell speeches. Already the villagers were setting tables outside and a large goat was hanging over a fire. It sizzled as the hair was burned from its hide and the roasting began.

The entire family returned with me in the afternoon. The head table stood off alone in front of the villagers. We were the first served with heaping individual bowls of rice and goat meat. Each bowl gave off a sickly unpleasant smell. My daughter, Christy, sitting beside me spoke up in all honesty, as children are apt to do, "Daddy it stinks," she said. I agreed, but cautioned her to keep her comments to herself.

Then my wife, Joan, asked, "Harry what are we going to do?" Apparently, as the entire goat was roasted over the fire, its bowel had ruptured during cooking. The contents of the bowel became the seasoning and gave the meat its pungent aroma. I suggested they all begin with the rice and chew on a portion of the hide. "Ka tabawa abinci da ni," I reminded them. "Touch food with me." This African custom saved us as our appetites were very small. We knew that whatever was left in our bowls would gladly be eaten by others. We knew that no offense would be taken at the food we left for that only indicated we were satisfied. Actually, the meat did not taste bad; it was just getting past its aroma.

In spite of the cooking accident, I was honored by the celebration and the warm appreciation shown to us. It was humbling and made saying goodbye even more difficult.

"But as he left he promised, 'I will come back if it is God' will...'" (Acts 18:21) We had not yet made a decision about returning and were leaving it in God's hand and direction. Do you seek God's will for your life? When you pray, "thy will be done," do you mean it? Or are your will and desires still more important?

JOURNEY HOME

"Do not forget to entertain strangers,
for by so doing some people have entertained
angels without knowing it."

HEBREWS 13:2

The last six weeks sped by quickly. Today we begin our trip home and Gord is flying all six of us in the small plane to Lagos. We landed in a field on the outskirts of the city. The grassy field looked like a vacant lot; it was isolated and surrounded by a low wire fence. It was deserted and without buildings except for a phone booth at one end of the field. We called for a taxi and then rode to the wharf where our ship, the *Aureol*, was docked. Three strong bare-chested young Africans hoisted our luggage atop their heads and began rapidly walking down the crowded wharf toward our ship; Christy and I kept pace as best we could trying to keep the receding luggage in sight. Joan, with the smaller children, proceeded more slowly.

We spent the next seven days at sea making our way up the West Coast of Africa and finally to the Canary Islands. The ship stopped at three ports along the West African coast to pick up mail and cargo. The voyage was restful and refreshing. The food was a real treat after the years in the bush of Africa. The weather in the Canary Islands turned cool and rainy, but two days later we made the short flight to Spain. There were no metal detectors or body imaging machines at the airport, but all the male and female passengers were separated into two lines. Each passenger was hand searched and patted down before entering the aircraft. What an aircraft it was, a brand new 747. We had only heard about this plane, but had never previously seen one.

After boarding the aircraft, we were assigned to one of the forward compartments. To our surprise, we were the only passengers among the fifty seats there. We all stretched out over several seats and were quickly asleep. As we approached Kennedy airport in New York, our anxiety grew. We still had to catch another flight at LaGuardia across the busy city. Joan and I still had some unhappy memories of our arrival in Florida, six years previous, and the hassle with customs. We prayed we could pass through customs quickly.

I have never seen an angel, but as we entered the crowded customs area I heard a loud voice above the crowd noise, "Sudan United Mission, Sudan United Mission over here." Looking across the room, I saw a man waving briskly at us. How did he know we were missionaries? We rapidly pushed our luggage cart toward him and the door he was holding open to the street. Customs officials never glanced at us or examined our passports or luggage. We moved unheeded to the street outside. A taxi waited at the curb with the door open for us. I "tipped the baggage handler," and we were soon on the LaGuardia flight home.

"Do not forget to entertain strangers, for by so doing some people have entertained angels without knowing it." (Hebrews 13:2) Do you entertain strangers? Have you ever entertained an angel? "Are not all angels ministering spirits sent to serve those who will inherit salvation?" Hebrews 1:14 I know we met one.

Sunday worship, New church Jenowa Gida

POINT OF VIEW

"So from now on we regard no one
from a worldly point of view..."

2 CORINTHIANS 5:16

It has been my lifelong habit to ask God each night to give me an opportunity to speak with someone each day, someone who needs comfort, assurance, or God's plan of salvation. I have been amazed throughout my life at the daily opportunities presented to me. Opportunities that came at the most unexpected times and often from people from whom I least expected it.

Throughout my career, I have had the privilege of interacting with individuals from every walk of life and every economic status. They have come from every educational background including those with little formal education. They have come from different cultures and different social strata. Some were criminals and people of ill repute. Others were addicted to drugs or alcohol. Some were in prison. How do you view those around you? Are they quickly categorized as to whether you would even speak to them or people you would just totally avoid? Do you view everyone from a worldly point of view?

The world has many classifications for people. At the top are usually those with money, celebrity status, star athletes, and performers. For many, they can do no wrong no matter their behavior or how poor their relationships with others. Then there are those with positions of authority and power or those from whom we expect to receive some benefit. From them we also, at times, excuse extremes of behavior. Finally, there are the outcasts, the poor, the uneducated, the homeless, the alcoholics, the drug addicts, the single mothers, the prostitutes, and the criminals. Do you view everyone from a worldly point of view?

The Apostle Paul said in this passage from Corinthians that he too once viewed , even Christ, from a worldly point of view. When he met Christ he could no longer view anyone in that way. Christ, who ate with tax collectors, publicans, and sinners. Christ who forgave the adulterous woman. We, like Paul, should no longer view people from a worldly point of view, but attempt to see them with the eyes of Christ.

PROSTITUTE

"so from now on...we regard no one
from a worldly point of view..."

2 CORINTHIANS 5:16

The woman had been a prostitute for many years. She became my patient when I was the doctor on call in the emergency room at Porter Memorial Hospital in Valparaiso, Indiana. The doctor on call was responsible for patients in the emergency room who did not have a personal physician. My office, in Demotte, Indiana, was twenty-one miles from the hospital. In 1978 there were no emergency room physicians, and each physician was responsible for providing emergency care for his or her patients. When the hospital called, I gave the nurse initial orders and, as soon as possible, drove to the hospital to care for her.

Over the next three years, I saw her in the emergency room on average of two to three times each year. Whenever she became ill, she would present herself to the emergency room and tell them that Dr. Holwerda was her physician. She never appeared at my office.

One day, she became severely ill with a fever and infection. I drove to the emergency room and admitted her to the hospital. The day before discharge, I made her my last patient of the morning. When I reached her room, I sat down on a chair beside her bed. I asked questions, and we quietly discussed her life from before college until now. Her mother, she said, was a religious fanatic who preached God's law. From her comments it was obvious her mother never spoke of God's love or grace. Her mother's lack of grace drove her from wanting anything to do with the church or religion. She tried to disobey God's laws in any way possible. She acted out in a sexual manner at any opportunity, and then came her life of prostitution.

I told her there were three things she had to understand to find comfort in God's love.

First, how great her sins were, second, how Christ could deliver her, and third, how she could live a life of gratitude to God. I did not feel it necessary to talk to her about sin. She was very well aware of it. Her problem was that she didn't believe God could forgive her. I asked her if during the three years of our doctor/patient relationship, she ever felt I had treated her with anything other than kindness or respect. She said never. I then reminded her that I was a sinner as well and if I could forgive her, certainly God would. We prayed.

Six weeks later my secretary walked into my office with a small envelope. "Doc, you have to read this," she said. Inside was a small check for ten dollars and a short note. The note indicated that she had left the area and moved back with relatives in Michigan. In a postscript she added, "Thank you, for showing me the love of God. "I no longer view anyone from a worldly point of view."

THE PRISON

"...'I was in prison and you came to visit me'.
When did we see you sick or in prison and go to
visit you?' The King will reply, 'I tell you the truth,
whatever you did for one of the least of these brothers
of mine, you did for me.'"

MATTHEW 25:36, 39, 40

A few years after retirement, I received a letter from a private medical group. They were in charge of medical care in the State of Michigan prisons. They were in need of more physicians. It sounded intriguing. I was interviewed, but before accepting the position, I met the recruiter at the prison where I was to be assigned.

Have you ever been in a prison? The position I was offered was in a high security prison. It was formidable even from the parking lot. Seven large brick buildings surrounded a large courtyard. Six gun towers were strategically placed around the perimeter. The towers gave the rifleman inside an open view of the spaces between the buildings and the center courtyard. The entire complex was wrapped with a double row of 12-foot fences. Each fence, in turn, was wrapped with large rolls of razor wire, from top to bottom, inside and out. Each razor on the wire was at least three inches in length. No one had ever escaped from inside. Multiple tall light poles were spaced to instantly turn night into day.

We entered through the only entrance. It took a state identification card and an officer's pat down to enter the first of a series of heavy steel doors. Each clanged loudly as it closed, leaving you isolated in the small space before the next door. Each set of doors was controlled by an officer who viewed you from a separate secure space.

Following my tour of the medical clinic, we walked to a building isolating a hundred of the prison's worst inmates. Each occupied a sparse cell where a solid steel front prevented the prisoner from seeing others. There was a small window with 4-inch thick glass that allowed a view of the inside of the cellblock. It was also covered by a steel door that could be opened or closed at the guard's discretion. The cells were in two double-tiered wings. The noise that echoed from the cells was a cacophony of shouting and screams. The noise was punctuated by every filthy word and expression known to man. It was intimidating and frightening. As I was led to one of the cells I uttered a silent prayer, "Lord, if you want me to stay and work here, you will have to take away my fear."

I opened the small steel door covering the thick glass window in one of the cells. The prisoner was twenty-six years old. I greeted him and he pathetically described the contents of his "home." He told me his early release date was 2046. It was then that God suddenly removed my fear and replaced it with compassion. Throughout the following year, despite multiple stabbings, violent language, monthly beatings, and the threatening appearance of the inmates, by God's grace my fear was gone.

"...I was in prison and you came to visit me." (Matthew 25:36) Have you ever done so? Will you?

Pastor and Elder leading aged man for baptism

Pilot Gord Buys

A DIFFERENT KIND OF CAT

"So from now on we regard no one from a
worldly point of view. Though we once regarded
Christ in this way, we do so no longer. Therefore,
if anyone is in Christ, he is a new creation,
the old has gone, the new has come..."

2 CORINTHIANS 5:16-17

During my two weeks of orientation, I was saddened by the attitude of some members of the medical clinic and some of the prison guards. They had no respect for the humanity of the prisoners. Some verbally cursed them and others sought to do as little as possible for them. Some of my training physicians regarded the prisoners as if they carried the plague and would not think of touching them without wearing rubber gloves.

I resolved to courteously greet each prisoner in my office and to offer a handshake. It was not an approval of what they had done, but a recognition that they were still human beings. I often said to them I believe you are still one of God's children, just a disobedient one.

I can still see the face of my first patient. He was a tall middle-aged black male from Detroit. He walked briskly through the door and approached my desk. I greeted him with a good morning and standing behind my desk extended my hand. He paused and stood looking at my hand for what seemed a long time. Then a broad smile creased his face and he firmly gave me the full inner-city handshake. "Doc," he said, "no one has shaken my hand in medical care in fifteen years." Within days new prisoners coming into the clinic said to me, "Doc, the word in the yard is that you are ok." Soon the handshake was expected and many wished one before leaving the office as well.

Months later the leader of the Aryan gang sat with me in my office. As we chatted about my relationship with him and the other prisoners, he asked a question and made an observation. "Do you remember when I first walked in here eleven months ago? You stood up and stuck out your hand. I said to myself, this is a different kind of cat. Nobody shakes hands here Doc. Everyone is always on their guard. You blew us away! We never open up and I opened up to you on our very first meeting." A different kind of cat. The Apostle Paul said we are new creatures. It was for me a humbling exegesis.

"So from now on we regard no one from a worldly point of view... Therefore, if anyone is in Christ, he is a new creation..." (II Corinthians 5:16-17) Are you in Christ? Then you are a new creation; a different kind of cat. Is it evident to those with whom you interact each day?

CHRIST'S AMBASSADORS

"So from now on we regard no one from a worldly point of view. Though we once regarded Christ in this way, we do so no longer. Therefore, if anyone is in Christ, he is a new creation... We are therefore Christ's ambassadors, as though God were making his appeal through us. We implore you on Christ's behalf: Be reconciled to God."

2 CORINTHIANS 5:16, 17, 20

Along with the handshake, I also offered a small business sized card with the first two questions and answers from the Heidelberg Catechism:

Q&A 1. What is your only comfort in life and in death? That I am not my own but belong to a faithful Savior Jesus Christ. He has fully paid for all my sins with His precious blood and set me free from the tyranny of the devil. He also watches over me in such a way that not a hair can fall from my head without the will of my Father in heaven: in fact all things must work together for my salvation. Because I belong to Him, Christ, by His Holy Spirit assures me of eternal life and makes me whole heartedly willing and ready from now on to live for Him.

Q&A 2. What must you know to live and die in the joy of this comfort? Three things: first how great my sin and misery are; second, how I am set free from all my sins and misery; third, how I am to thank God for such a deliverance.

Almost daily there were wonderful conversations with a few of the prisoners about their lives, future, and relationship to God. We talked a lot about God's undeserved favor or as it is known in church "Grace". One prisoner as we read the card together, stopped me at the line describing, "His precious blood." He tapped his chest with the card and said, "Doc, that precious blood gives me goose-bumps."

Many of the prisoners related how they shared and copied the card for their bunkmates. Others read it to their family members during their monthly phone call. Toward the end of the year a fifty-eight year old inmate came to my office for care. He appeared much older yet he was twelve years my junior. He had been severely beaten by a younger cellmate a few days earlier over a TV dispute. A favorite prison weapon is the padlock from each prisoner's foot locker. Placed in a sock and swung it will easily break facial bones. His cellmate was careful to beat him below the shoulders so that the officers would not notice. He was literally black and blue from his shoulders to his waist. After I had tended to his medical needs, he sat down by my desk. "Doc," he said. "I have something important to show you." He then pulled out his wallet and removed the catechism card I had given him. Holding it up, he said. "Doc do you remember giving me this card four months ago? I read it every day and it gives me a lot of comfort and I believe He is coming again!"

Christ Ambassadors… are you? Do you share the Good News of reconciliation with God? It is, "…as though God were making his appeal through you. We (I) implore you on Christ's behalf: Be reconciled to God." (II Corinthians 5:20)

RESPECT

"...make it your ambition to lead a quiet life:
You should mind your own business and work with
your hands, just as we told you, so that your daily
life may win the respect of outsiders..."

1 THESSALONIANS 4:11-12

I had asked God to remove my fear on my first visit to the prison and He had done so. He filled me with compassion and the prisoners were a blessing. During the year there were eight stabbings in the yard, officers were attacked nearly every month, and one nurse was beaten never to return.

The respect I gave to the prisoners with a handshake was returned to me 1,000 fold. Each day, I walked to the various prison buildings among the prisoners in the yard. They were not permitted to stop me although many wanted to talk. Despite all the violence around me, I was never threatened. Numerous greetings were shouted daily from all over the yard, but the most frequent was a quiet "God bless" as I walked beside them.

One morning, I was utterly surprised by a prisoner's response. He was a giant of a man. He stood over 6 feet, 8 inches tall and must have weighed over 350 pounds. I took care of his medical problems, but we had not had a spiritual chat. When I had finished, he rose to leave, towering over my desk. Instead of turning to go, he reached back toward me. For a moment I wondered what was going to happen as he placed both of his hands on mine. Then he quietly said, "The Lord bless you and keep you, the Lord cause his face to shine upon you and give you peace." Then he turned and left the room.

The isolation cellblock, which had so frightened me on my first day, was now a different place. By regulation, I had to visit the cellblock once every two weeks. I had to inspect each prisoner in his cell, viewing and talking with him through the small window. This inspection was primarily to evaluate each prisoner for signs of psychiatric stress, starvation, or suicidal impulses. It was now much quieter than on my first day. Now, as I began my rounds someone would shout, "Doc's on the rock." Immediately, the place became quieter and I could talk with each inmate without shouting.

Two weeks before leaving the prison, I had a final visit with an elderly black prisoner. We had shared our faith extensively over the past year. He was so grateful for the Catechism card. He read it faithfully and shared it with anyone who would listen. I was saddened to tell him my year in the prison was nearly finished. He was comforting. "It is ok Doc," he said. "It is not how long you stay; it's what kind of legacy you leave. You brought the Light into this cold, dark, evil place. That is what we will remember."

SOLI DEO GLORIA